Taking Liberties

Seán Enright and James Morton

Taking Liberties

The Criminal Jury in the 1990s

Weidenfeld and Nicolson · *London*

George Weidenfeld and Nicolson Ltd
91 Clapham High Street, London SW4 7TA

ISBN 0 297 82029 X

Printed in Great Britain at The Bath Press, Avon

Contents

Acknowledgements

The notion that the jury is under threat and in decline is not new. The first signs were charted by Lord Devlin (*Trial by Jury*) and Cornish (*The Jury*); much more recently this trend has been discussed by Findley and Duff (*The Jury Under Attack*). Pride of place perhaps ought to go to Harman and Griffiths (*Justice Deserted*) for taking an unequivocal stand when few were prepared to listen. Much has happened since Harman and Griffiths were writing in 1979; certainly it is now clear that the debate over the future of the jury is reaching a critical stage and we hope this book will make a useful contribution.

We would like to take this opportunity to thank all those individuals who helped in the writing of this book. In particular, we owe a debt to Lorna Cameron and Hilary Bateson for advice, encouragement, typing, proof-reading, and editing seemingly endless drafts of the manuscript, and to Tony Radevsky for reading the manuscript and making numerous helpful suggestions. Thanks are due to J. M. E. Robinson for research assistance in relation to the jury system in Hong Kong and Australia.

So far as history is concerned we have relied mainly on *A History of English Law* (Holdsworth), *Trial by Jury* (Devlin), *The Jury* (Cornish), *Verdict According to Conscience* (Green), and *State Trials*.

On the history of interference with juries we have relied on *Elements in the Art of Packing* (Bentham) and the various works of E. P. Thompson. In Chapter 3, which deals with the subject of vetting, we have been influenced by *Justice Deserted* (Harman & Griffiths), *The Frontiers of Secrecy* (David Leigh), *Jury on Trial* (Freeman), and *Stand-by for the Crown* (McEldowney). We are grateful to Stuart Bell (for providing the Bettaney letter), Alf Dubs (for providing The Jury Vetting (Abolition) Bill), and Brian Sedgemore for taking the time to provide some background information on the subject of vetting. The Attorney-General has kindly granted permission to reprint the Guidelines on Jury Vetting and the exercise of the Crown stand-by.

On the suspension of jury trial in Northern Ireland we found *Civil Liberties* (Messrs Bailey, Harris, and Jones) to be a useful fund of reference material. We were also influenced by *Ten Years On* (Messrs Boyle, Hadden, and Hillyard) and *Abolishing the Diplock Courts* (S. C. Greer and A. White) on which we have relied in relation to the incidence of perverse verdicts and juror intimidation in Northern Ireland in the early 1970s.

Finally, we are obliged to all those authors who gave consent to their work being quoted, and we are grateful to Her Majesty's Stationery Office for the permission to quote from various Government reports.

The opinions expressed in this book are solely our own as are any errors. The law is as stated on August 1, 1989.

Seán Enright & James Morton

Introduction

This is a book about the future of the jury in criminal trials, a future that, almost daily, seems far less secure than it did twenty years ago. We hope that, like Caesar who was said to be all things to all men, this text will prove to be the same. We hope that it will claim the attention of lawyers and sociologists and that it will provide a guide to those with more than a passing interest in the criminal justice system, how it operates in this country, and the direction in which it is going at the present time.

The subject of the jury system has become controversial and, save for a few honourable scholarly exceptions,[1] much of the vast body of literature on the subject can be described as partisan. Whilst we trust our text is relatively dispassionate we cannot pretend other than that our own strong inclination is in favour of the concept of trial by jury. We hope, nevertheless, that the book will provide a balanced account, showing the 'warts and all' which grow on the system rather than attempting to present an unblemished skin.

We take as our starting point the proposition that society is undergoing a major crisis of confidence in the jury system. Trial by jury has after all become something of a rarity in civil cases. The 1989 end of term listing statement issued by the High Court indicated that the backlog of jury trials in civil cases was a mere one hundred and five. The bulk of these were defamation cases and the balance, about seventeen per cent, were actions brought against the police for assault, false imprisonment or malicious prosecution. In the Coroner's Court the use of the jury has been on the wane for many years. The Criminal Law Act of 1977 greatly contributed to this process by restricting the kinds of cases which necessitate the summoning of an inquest jury. And in 1980 Parliament abolished the modest if inconvenient and sometimes embarrassing right of the inquest jury to add a rider to its verdict.

In criminal cases some 97% of the work is dealt with by magistrates.[2] The remaining 3% of cases are committed to the Crown Court but that does not mean they are actually dealt with by a judge and jury. Most of those committed plead guilty without a jury ever being sworn.

At one time the right to a jury trial was considered a basic freedom and had attained a status of almost mythical proportion; now it has become reserved for only the most serious contested criminal trials. In 1956 Lord Devlin was expressing the common consensus about the jury when he wrote that: 'No tyrant could afford to leave a subject's freedom in the hands of twelve of his countrymen.'[3]

Today in Britain Lord Devlin's views would not necessarily find the same broad acceptance. The reputation of the jury as a barrier against oppressive laws has been seriously questioned.[4] Other, long perceived notions of the jury as a barometer of social attitudes, or as an impartial tribunal of fact, have been doubted, and even derided by lawyers,[5] politicians, academics,[6] and the press alike. An extreme, and perhaps not wholly disinterested, attitude is reflected in the view of the Justices' Clerks Society: '. . . lawyers will advise clients to elect jury trial in cases where there exists no credible defence in the hope that there will be returned a perverse verdict'.[7]

Dissatisfaction with the jury system has tended to be voiced in an increasingly strident manner. In its crudest and most extreme form it has been said that there are too many 'acquittals by juries made up of the unemployed, the lower working classes, and housewives'.[8] Had the comment not been made by a Member of Parliament it might not require rebuttal. For the present we would say that empirical evidence does not, in general, bear out the suggestion that acquittal rates in the United Kingdom are affected by the ethnic or social composition of juries.[9]

In recent years the more strident criticism has tended to hamper discussion of the issues. It is a trend which is attributable undoubtedly, at least in part, to the implementation of the Criminal Justice Act 1972 which brought the qualification for jury service broadly into line with the right to vote. Michael Freeman, Professor of Law at University College, London, writes: 'It is surely no coincidence that attacks upon the jury should have increased with the abolition of the property qualification for jury service.'[10]

But it is not just since the 1972 Act that this criticism has been voiced. The belief that juries acquit too readily has been expressed both before and after 1972, notably by Sir Robert Mark, again a not wholly disinterested party. Charges of bias, cowardice, and gullibility in jurors abound, a particular instance being the so-called 'Cyprus Spy Trial' in 1985. It was in this case that defence counsel were said to have banded together to use the peremptory challenge to obtain a jury-box full of those most likely not merely to be sympathetic to their clients but most hostile to the Crown. This may or may not have been correct but it was a watershed in the campaign to abolish the peremptory challenge.

Others have argued that since juries are comprised of a random cross-section of society, it is inherently unlikely that juries are able to discharge their functions in all but the simplest of cases. Professor Glanville Williams put the argument against the jury system most succinctly: 'There is no guarantee that members of a particular jury may not be quite unusually ignorant, credulous, slow witted, narrowminded, biased or temperamental'.[11] Quite so; in fact the very criticisms which are regularly, if sometimes unfairly, applied to certain judges, and some members of the stipendiary and lay magistracy. On a more measured note, the Roskill Fraud Trial Committee Report, in recommending the abolition of jury trial in complex fraud cases, took the view that '. . . too many jurors are out of their depth'.[12]

Another current attack on the jury system relates to the possibility of 'nobbling'. Much of the emphasis has been placed on the vulnerability of jurors to threats and particularly their susceptibility to bribery rather than on ways to deal with the perpetrators without diminishing the rights of defendants. It was in just such an atmosphere that majority verdicts were introduced in 1967[13] and jury trial suspended for terrorist cases in Northern Ireland in 1973.[14]

There are those who argue (like G. K. Chesterton over a different issue) that the expense is damnable. It is said that the cost of jury trial is disproportionate to the issues at stake in so-called minor offences, and that such cases ought not to be tried before a jury but before magistrates. The former Lord Chancellor, Lord Hailsham, frequently advocated that cases of petty theft and dishonesty should only be triable summarily. It is an opinion shared by many of the judiciary; even as this book was being written the 900-strong Criminal

Bar Association was divided on the subject, with many powerful voices suggesting the time had come to remove the right of jury trial in cases of dishonest behaviour involving less than £250.

In 1973 the James Committee took a similar view; it had been set up to examine 'The Distribution of Criminal Business between the Crown Court and the Magistrates' Court', and although many of its recommendations were incorporated into the Criminal Law Bill 1977 the proposal to abolish jury trial for offences of theft of a value of less than £20 was shelved after strong opposition, although the right of the defendant to seek trial by jury for a number of other offences was abolished. We note in passing that the Criminal Justice Act 1988 has further eroded the right of trial by jury for so-called minor offences.

For centuries we have had a system which has allowed ordinary people an opportunity to participate in the process of criminal justice. Apart from the vote it is the only opportunity that many have to make a meaningful contribution to the running of the country. The system, however, depends for its efficacy upon a degree of trust in the honesty and competence of individual jurors. Unquestioning respect for the jury, if indeed it ever existed, is rightly a thing of the past. However, we seem to be far beyond that stage. A significant body of opinion in this country has neither the confidence in, nor sees the necessity for, the system as it now operates. The decline of the jury as a tribunal of fact over the last century is well established; but, much more importantly, in its most vital role as an arbiter between the prosecuting arm of the State and the individual, the jury system is being eroded far too freely and with insufficient consideration for the long-term consequences.

We propose to examine the evolution of the jury, and the recent developments in the law relating to juries in criminal trials. We shall attempt to explain the reasons for the changes that have occurred and to evaluate the effect they have had on the quality of justice in this country. We will consider the efficacy and desirability of jury trial in criminal cases and consider what reforms are necessary to ensure its survival as a viable mode of trial.

The first chapter examines the history of the jury to the present day. Chapter 2 chronicles the history of conflict between the State and jury, with particular reference to the lengths to which the executive arm of Government has gone to control individual juries. Chapter 3 examines one of the few remaining jury control mechanisms operated by the State: jury vetting. Until recently vetting was thought to be of historical interest only, but less than 20 years ago it was discovered, almost by accident, to be flourishing.

Closely related to vetting is the challenge which has been the subject of so much recent controversy and discontent. The curtailment and eventual abolition of the peremptory challenge will be examined in Chapter 4, where we also consider the future of the challenge for cause. Chapter 5 looks at one of the most remarkable reforms of the jury system: the abolition, in 1967, of the unanimous verdict. Did the suggested spate of nobbling make this reform necessary or was it merely a panic measure bolstered by dissatisfaction with acquittal rates?

As the use of the jury has declined there has been a corresponding rise in the power of the magistracy. Chapter 6 looks at the work of the 27,000 men and women who, with minimal training, decide both facts and sentence in the vast majority of criminal cases. Chapter 7 examines the work of the Roskill Committee, its recommendations regarding complex fraud cases and its proposals for the abolition of the jury in these trials. Chapter 8 looks at the situation in Northern Ireland where the Diplock Courts hold sway and where jury trial for scheduled offences has been suspended if not abolished altogether.

Chapter 9 discusses the pros and cons of jury trial and considers some of the alternatives. Finally, Chapter 10 looks at current problems relating to jury trial in England and Wales and suggests some reforms which could be made to ensure its improvement and survival.

Chapter 1

Origins

It is ironic that the bastion of the adversarial system, the jury, began its life with an inquisitorial function. As the name implies it relates to a man who has taken an oath. Introduced into England by the Norman kings it was used, initially, as a fact-finding body.[1] Invoking the name of God on the Bible was reckoned to be a grave matter, and it was believed that once sworn the juror would tell the truth. Therefore, if a number of jurors all swore to the same fact it must be correct. The jurors all came from the same place and could depose to what they actually knew of the case.

It was not for a century and a half that the jury became used in an adversarial process. Before then there had been a number of methods used to prove who was the better man and therefore right. Where there was a specific accuser trial by battle was one method, and indeed, one which remained on the statute books until 1819. Where there was no specific accuser but the defendant was accused of serious crime, and the accusation was by public notoriety, it was dealt with in the following way:

the accused is either imprisoned or finds sureties, then the truth of the matter shall be investigated by many and varied inquests and interrogations before the justices and arrived at by considering the probable facts and possible conjectures both for and against the accused who must, as a result, be either absolved or made to purge himself by ordeal.[2]

The procedure followed in a trial by ordeal usually involved a three-day fast after which the accused picked up a hot iron, walked three paces and put the iron down. The hand was bandaged and sealed and after a further three days the wound was inspected. If it was healing well that was deemed to be a sign from God in his favour. Other variations, all of which incorporated religious ceremonies, included the plunging of an accused's hand into a cauldron of boiling water to pull out a ring. There was also the ordeal of being bound and then laid on water. Curiously, if the accused sank he was deemed innocent; if he floated there was immediate proof of his guilt.

Of course the whole process was open to corruption: for example, weights could be added. Another method particularly lent itself to outside help. This was the *corsnaed* or cursed morsel. The accused had to swallow a piece of bread or cheese in which had been inserted a feather. If he choked there was the proof of his guilt.[3] It does not require much imagination to realise that the success or failure of this particular test would lie with the size of the feather (although in 1166, 600 men underwent the ordeal and were convicted). On the other hand, Maitland rather sourly wrote that between 1201 and 1219 he had only found one case where the trial by ordeal did not acquit the accused.[4]

By 1220 the trial by ordeal had lost its place to jury trial. A major factor in this transition was the influence of the Church. Clerical opposition to these practices came to a head in 1215 with the edict of Lateran, which condemned trial by ordeal and proscribed the role of the clergy in these ceremonies. It was now for the jury to fill the void created.

Early days

The initial use to which the jury was put, after being fact-finders, was as a jury of presentment. Indeed, in the later years of trial by ordeal a presentment jury had given a 'medial' judgement, deciding what type of ordeal should be used. Again, a jury could be summonsed to declare whether a charge was brought in good faith or out of malice. This was a major step in the development of the jury and its role in a criminal trial. If the jury was capable of working out whether the complaint had been brought maliciously, then it was quite capable of working out whether the accused was guilty or innocent.

From the end of the twelfth century the jury could accuse, after which the accused underwent the ordeal; it became not only presenter but trier of an accusation (with a number added to the initial 23

7

members to bring the total to anything between 24 and 84). Some judges did not bother to enlarge the presenting jury but, if there was a substantial number, it would be examined by units and the often conflicting results brought before the justices who then made up their own minds.

Although there had been the right to purchase from the Crown the right of trial by jury and so avoid trial by battle, there was also a degree of reluctance to condemn a man once he had been deprived of his right to trial by ordeal. In 1221 Thomas de la Herthe was presented by a Grand Jury as an associate of a felon, quaintly named Howe Golightly. There was some debate whether jury trial was lawful. Was it really due process? In the event the court held that he was entitled to a jury of 24 knights.

Once this precedent had been established the practice was to summon a large number of knights to take the responsibility for a decision or merely require the accused to find sureties. In a grave case, such as murder, it was still possible that all he would be required to do was abjure the realm. There were, of course, teething troubles. In the early days, for instance, the jury was not particularly well treated (a comment which might be made of today's jurors). The members of a jury of presentment which (in the next stage of the case having been metamorphosed into a jury to determine guilt or innocence) acquitted the accused, were liable to a fine. It is unsurprising that there were few acquittals. Nevertheless, many preferred it to trial by ordeal.

As late as 1346 a majority verdict could be obtained from this unwieldy entity, but by 1367 it was established that the verdict had to be unanimous. Accordingly, the trial jury was slimmed down to its present size of twelve. It would, of course, have been almost impossible to obtain a unanimous verdict from as many as 84. There have been many and varied suggestions as to why the number of twelve was chosen:

And first as to their (the jury's) number twelve: and this number is no less esteemed by our law than the Holy Writ. If the twelve apostles on their twelve thrones must try us in our eternal state, good reason hath the law to appoint the number of twelve to try our temporal. The tribes of Israel were twelve, and Solomon's officers were twelve (I Kings 4:7). Therefore, not only matters of fact were tried by twelve, but of ancient times twelve judges were to try matters in law in the Exchequer Chamber and there were twelve counsellors of state for matters of state; and he that wageth his law must have eleven others with him who believe he says true. And the law is so precise in this number of twelve that if the trial be by more or less, it is a mistrial.[5]

Lord Devlin, on the other hand, offers a suggestion both logical and wry:

It is clear that what was wanted was a number that was large enough to create a formidable body of opinion in favour of the side that won; and doubtless the reason for having twelve instead of ten, eleven or thirteen was much the same as gives twelve pennies to the shilling and which exhibits an early English abhorrence of the decimal system.[6]

As society became more complex the jury system developed to meet the problems that arose. For instance, by the sixteenth century the Coronor's jury had developed to resolve questions arising out of sudden or unexplained deaths.

By the eighteenth century special juries were being empanelled to try complex commercial cases. Special juries were also empanelled to try misdemeanours in the criminal courts. There were also other variants of the special jury; in criminal cases a woman convicted of a capital offence could avoid the death sentence by establishing that she was 'quick with child.' This issue would be determined by a jury of matrons. Also, from as early as the thirteenth century a foreign national could claim a jury *de medietate linguae*, that is, a jury composed of six English and six non Englishmen. Then there was the grand jury whose function it was to commit defendants for trial where the evidence amounted to a 'true bill'.

Maltreatment of jurors

Being a jury man was not very pleasant in these early days. Any member of a petty jury who had presented a person as suspected and then acquitted him was deemed to have contradicted himself and be liable to punishment. The idea that there might be a case to answer but that the material did not justify a conviction was slow to develop.

Additionally, any jury of that era would be well known to the defendant, his friends, and relatives and as such it was susceptible to bribery and inducement. To counter this a jury once sworn was not allowed to separate, nor was the jury allowed food or drink. Indeed, evidence that jurors had been given sustenance was once enough to render a verdict void. Sometimes it seemed that verdicts turned on a stubborn juror or a robust constitution. For instance, juryman Bates, on being told that there was to be no food until the verdict, against which he was holding out, was returned, declared that he would 'eat the ceiling' before convicting. From then on he was known in his parish as 'eat the ceiling' Bates. There is also the case of the portly juryman who vowed that he would hold out for an acquittal until he was 'no thicker than a pipe'.[7] The rule was eventually relaxed. Once the jury had returned a privy verdict, that is, a verdict in private amongst themselves, after the court had risen, it was allowed food and drink though it was still not permitted to separate until court reconvened the next morning.

Judges were by no means sympathetic towards jurors. In the case of Mercy Newton, on trial for matricide, the jury was unable to agree, locked up overnight, and still unable to agree a verdict the following day. One member fell ill and the doctor summoned said he should be given 'beef tea and brandy'. The doctor argued that the illness was due to 'exhaustion, because of the antique absurdity of denying all food to jurymen for the duration of their inquest'. The trial judge, Baron Rolfe, would have none of this asserting that a juryman should be given 'no nutriment which all might equally want, merely because he is weaker and less able to do without it'.[8]

Even as late as the nineteenth century, verdicts were being quashed whenever it was discovered that juries had been sent provisions. The scope of this rule was gradually relaxed so that verdicts were usually only quashed if it could be shown that the food and drink had been sent in by the plaintiff, defendant, or their respective supporters. In *Crooke* v. *Caunt* one juror smuggled in beer and the trial judge Byles J. then had to deal with a drunken jury. Eventually the law was changed in 1870 to allow the long suffering jurors to be fed and watered.[9]

If at the end of an assize, jurors had not reached a verdict in a particular case, they were likely to be taken along to the next town to continue their deliberations. Lord Campbell had this to say: 'At the assizes according to traditional law, a jury who can't agree ought to be kept locked up as long as the assizes last and be carried in a cart after the judge to the boundary of the next county and there be shot into a ditch.'[10]

This problem faced Baron Channell trying the case of Mary Harris and Charlotte Winsor for murder at the Exeter Assizes in 1865:

Darkness had long fallen, indeed it was a quarter past seven o'clock in the evening when they were locked up. The court continued to sit waiting for the verdict but the time passed by, and none was forthcoming. At half past eight the jury asked the judge to guide them more clearly on the subject of the medical evidence ... At ten minutes to eleven the judge inquired whether they were yet agreed on their verdict, and on the reply being in the negative, left them alone for a further three-quarters of an hour. At last, at twenty minutes to twelve he called up the jury once more, only to hear that they were still as far from agreement as before, and making no progress towards it. The judge now found himself in a dilemma. It was unusual to discharge a jury after less than five hours' consultation. On the other hand, the time was close upon midnight, and the next day was Sunday, which was not a day on which a judicial act could take place. If, then, the jury were locked up again, they would have to remain locked up all through Sunday, to their extreme discomfort. Nor could the verdict be given on Monday morning, because by that time he (the judge) was due to be opening the Assizes at Bodmin, in Cornwall, on the next stage of his circuit. Under all these circumstances Baron Channell resolved the dilemma by discharging the jury, but remanding the two prisoners in custody, to await a second trial at the summer assizes in July. This was unfortunate for Charlotte Winsor, at any rate, since it became known that eight out of the twelve jurors had favoured acquittal – and she was never again to come so near to escaping from the law's clutches.[11]

Doing without food and water was not the only deprivation a juryman could suffer. In late medieval times a jury which showed any signs of impartiality was either bribed or threatened. In the reign of Richard II one jury which gave a verdict of acquittal was so terrorised by the trial judge that it tried to retract its verdict and then had the worst of both worlds by not being allowed to do so.[12]

Struggling for independence

Jurors acting in their capacity of witnesses of fact who returned a perverse verdict in civil cases were deemed to have committed something akin to perjury, and a writ of attaint could be issued against them. In criminal cases, the verdict of a grand assize jury would stand, but the perjured jurymen could lose their chattels, be imprisoned and 'be accounted infamous'. Revealing the jury's secrets was no less a crime. In Edward III's reign a juryman who revealed matters which had come before him in his capacity as a grand juryman was indicted for felony and there was some argument that he could have been indicted for treason.[13]

The Court of the Star Chamber refined the practices of dealing with recalcitrant jurors. Any verdict against what was thought to be the weight of the evidence was treated as contempt of court. In Throckmorton's case, in 1554, the acquittal by the jury was followed by its members being imprisoned and fined. In the reigns of Henry VII and VIII, Queen Mary, and the early years of Elizabeth I, it was lamented that scarcely a term passed without some jury being fined for acquitting felons and murderers.[14] It was not until after the Restoration that the law came round to the view that only a corrupt verdict should be punished. By then, however, there had been some outstanding instances of jury defiance.[15]

No jury would convict John Lilburne, the leader of the Levellers, in 1649. A self-educated orator and pamphleteer, Lilburne was a self-appointed champion of the rights of common men. 'Freeborn John' first came to prominence before the Civil War when he was sentenced by the King's Court of Star Chamber to be whipped for publishing allegedly heretical pamphlets. He later served with distinction in Cromwell's New Model army, rising from private to lieutenant-colonel before being wounded and captured at Brentford. Sentenced to death he was spared by the threats of reprisals on loyalist prisoners.

In the aftermath of the war Lilburne became a vociferous opponent of the 'new tyranny' under Cromwell. This virulent opposition led to his trial and acquittal on a charge of treason in 1649. Shortly afterwards his political activities led Parliament to pass an Act exiling him and decreeing that his re-entry into the jurisdiction would be punishable by death. Lilburne, however, did return to England in June 1653 and was arrested. He was tried at the Old Bailey in August of that year for being within the jurisdiction contrary to statute. A letter which survives gives the flavour of the trial:

> Last week, John Lilburne was five times at his trial at the Sessions House, where he most courageously defended himself from Mr Steele, the Recorder ... Cromwell thought this fellow so considerable that during the time of his trial he kept three regiments continually in arms about St James.

Lilburne appealed to the jury over the head of the judge. He brazenly denied that he was the John Lilburne named in the indictment and asked the jury to consider the legitimacy of the statute passed against him, and required them to consider themselves 'equal judges of law and fact'. Despite the hostility of the judge, the jury acquitted Lilburne.

The verdict, described as a 'manifestation of strong anti-Government feeling among the populace of London at the time', was more than that. It was a courageous act which demonstrated an ability to stand firm against oppression. The jurors, who included woollen drapers, haberdashers, a book binder, and a tallow chandler, were not men of substance or influence. The following day the enormity of their decision was brought home to them. By an order of Parliament they were directed to appear before the Council of State to explain their verdict. They had defied the trial judge; they had defied the might of the State; now they were being called to account.

The examination of the jurors before the Council provides a unique insight into the changing attitudes to the jury and, in particular, to the jurors' perception of their function. Significantly only eleven jurors attended the examination. We may safely assume that the twelfth knew his presence was required but exercised discretion and made himself scarce.

On the morning of the examination the eleven jurors met secretly and with some trepidation at the Windmill Tavern, Coleman Street, no doubt to decide what answer to make to the Council. On examination, the foreman, Thomas Greene, avowed that he 'did discharge his conscience'. This was a phrase echoed by five of his fellow jurors (Tunman, Stephens, Hitchcock, Tomlins, and Evershot). It is a significant turn of phrase since it implies a willingness to disregard the letter of the law or the directions of the judge. Three jurors were persuaded to the view that 'jurors were equal judges of law and fact'; a notion which allowed them (Rayner, Gayne, and Stephens) to assess the validity of the statute upon which the prosecution was brought. Their observations are significant since this strand of thought was one which appears and reappears in an attenuated form until well into the eighteenth century. Three jurors (Hunt, Tomlins, and Owen) stated that they were not satisfied that the defendant was the John Lilburne named in the indictment. In fact this seems very unlikely and was probably more of a sop to the Council. Two jurors (Smith and Evershot) attended the examination but stoutly declined to debate the evidence with their interrogators.[16]

Probably because of Lilburne's popularity at the time, but nevertheless somewhat surprisingly, the jurors were neither fined nor imprisoned. Perhaps any punishment would have been too reminiscent of the absolute power exercised by the monarchy only a few years before. In any event the trial and the subsequent examination of the jurors prompted much popular debate. Here indeed lies the true significance of the trial. It effected a widespread change in the perception of the role of the jury; and the different views of the jurors themselves reflected ambivalent and changing attitudes to authority.

Of course, the notion that jurors were equal judges of fact and law did not appeal to the judiciary which gave short shrift to the proposition. From this moment on judge and jury were often in conflict, particularly in relation to the prosecutions of Quakers for practising their religion.

Another, less successful, effort by a jury was the trial of Dame Alice Lisle for high treason, at the Assizes at Winchester in August 1685 before the infamous Judge Jeffreys. She had sheltered two Nonconformists, John Hickes and Richard Nelthorpe, both supporters of Monmouth. Three times the jury refused to return a verdict of guilty and three times Jeffreys sent them back. Jeffreys had summed up for a verdict of guilt and expressed surprise when the jury even left the bar. It must have taken a good deal of courage to hold out as long as they did against the judge:

Foreman – My lord, we have one thing to beg of your lordship some directions in, before we can give our verdict in this case; we have some doubt upon whether there be sufficient proof that she knew Hicks to have been in the army.
Lord Chief Justice – There is as full proof as full proof can be; but you are the judges of the proof, for my part I thought there was no difficulty in it.
Foreman – My lord, we are in some doubt of it.
Lord Chief Justice – I cannot help your doubts . . .
Foreman – But my lord, we are not satisfied that she had notice that Hicks was in the army.
Lord Chief Justice – I cannot tell what would satisfy you . . . Come, come, gentlemen, it is a plain proof.
Foreman – My lord, we do not remember it was proved that she did ask any such question when they were there.
Lord Chief Justice – Sure you do not remember anything that has passed!

After they had returned a verdict of guilty the jurors were treated to a little homily:

Gentlemen, I did not think I should have had any occasion to speak after your verdict; but, finding some hesitancy and doubt among you, I cannot but say I wonder it should come about; for I think in my conscience the evidence was as full and plain as could be, and if I had been among you, and she had been my own mother, I should have found her guilty.[17]

All in all it was not that dissimilar to some trials of the present day when the jury which has returned a verdict contrary to the hopes and expectations of the trial judge is required to listen to a list of the accused's previous convictions or a tirade from the Bench.

Braver still were the jurors in the case of Penn and Mead, the Quakers. William Penn and William Mead were tried at the Old Bailey for Preaching in Gracechurch Street in contravention of a statute designed to suppress Nonconformist religions. The judge was determined to have a guilty verdict and the jury was called back from the jury-room, bullied and harangued. They acquitted Mead and could not agree about Penn. The recorder ordered the jury to be locked up for the night 'without meat, drink, fire, and tobacco'. And, by one account, refused a chamber-pot.[18] 'We shall have a verdict by the help of God or you shall starve for it', said the recorder. The jury held firm and three nights later acquitted Penn.

Onlookers at the trial say the verdict was to 'the great satisfaction of the assembly'. The judge's anger became plain to all: 'I am sorry, gentlemen, you have followed your own judgements and opinions, rather than the good and wholesome advice which was given you. God keep my life out of your hands, but for this the court fines you 40 marks a man; and imprisonment till paid.'

All twelve went to Newgate. Four jurors, including the foreman, Bushell, refused to pay and spent some months in gaol themselves before Bushell took the matter to appeal by way of a writ of habeas corpus. The appeal was heard by the Lord Chief Justice Vaughan who released them declaring 'the right of juries to give their verdict by their conscience'.

It is, however, only fair to add that juries did not always behave so well. In 1737 jurors were found in contempt for 'hustling halfpennies in a hat to determine their verdict'. In *Smith* v. *Great Northern Railway* in 1858 the jury reached a verdict by playing pitch and toss. (Possibly this was a reprisal for being locked up overnight.) One of their number had been taken ill and he alone was allowed half a pint of port wine and a few sandwiches to see him through until morning.[19]

Transition

In the seventeenth and eighteenth centuries the jury was still a local creature drawn from parishes. Jurors still had personal knowledge of the accused and complainant. In one case a speedy decision was given for the plaintiff on an issue of hard swearing. The jury was asked how the decision had been reached. 'I don't know the plaintiff but the defendant is a friend of mine, and I know he is a liar', said one juror; proving that even in those days jurors could divorce friendship from fact.[20]

Gradually it became accepted that jurors did not have to have personal knowledge of those involved. Pickpockets accused of theft on stage coaches could be tried in any county along the route through which the coach had passed[21]; and in 1856 Parliament accepted that if it was feared a local jury would not be impartial the trial could be moved to the central criminal court.[22] In due course knowledge by a juror of one of the parties became a ground for a challenge for cause.

Trial process and procedure

Until well into the nineteenth century trials could often be rowdy, ill-disciplined affairs with the judge often taking an active and partisan role. They sometimes combined extremes of pomp and ceremony with an engaging lack of forelock tugging by the participants. Jurors and witnesses would intervene in trials in a way that would not now be countenanced.

Jurors often deliberated without leaving the court-room. In ordinary criminal trials they often exercised a real degree of clemency towards the defendants; a process which more often than not meant ignoring the terms of their oath, sometimes with the connivance of the trial judge or at his instigation.

The defendant's role was limited and difficult. Until 1649 a defendant had neither the right to counsel nor to a copy of the indictment. The defendant, although he could make a statement from the dock, could not give any evidence at all until 1898.

The presence of the jury became a factor in the relaxation of some of the stricter rules of evidence and helped to shape others. For instance, the rules relating to hearsay confessions and corroboration are in part a response to the presence of a lay tribunal in the trial process.

The modern jury

By the twentieth century the jury had settled down into a 'male, middle-aged, middle-minded and middle-class' affair[23] which did not appeal to everyone. D.N. Pritt commented:

> ... juries have kept their reputation as defenders of popular liberty long after they ceased to merit it ... The law seems designed to secure that juries shall be drawn almost entirely from the middle and lower-middle classes, the very sections of the community most impervious not merely to new or unpopular ideas but even to the notion that such ideas ought to have a hearing.[24]

This was not an isolated view. A quarter of a century earlier the Mersey Committee had received evidence of anti-working-class bias in juries.[25]

This was in part due to the uniform national property qualification laid down in 1825,[26] which brought order to the ad hoc system of juror selection. The new Act extended the right to sit as a juror but it perpetuated the system of excluding the lower classes. An upper age limit had been fixed at sixty, and later raised to sixty-five. The upper age limit is now seventy although jurors of sixty-five or more can be excused as of right. The lower age limit of twenty-one was lowered to eighteen in 1972 when the property qualification was abolished.

The property qualification might seem to have been derisory but that is to disregard inflation. The property qualification had been fixed at owning freehold with an annual value of £10 or more, or a leasehold of not less than 21 years and of an annual value of £20 or more. For those who owned neither freehold nor medium-term leasehold property one had to be the occupier of a house with a rateable value of £30 in London and Middlesex, or £20 elsewhere, or in 'a house containing not less than fifteen windows'. This effectively disqualified adult children, wives, and lodgers. Additionally, since even as late as the 1950s many properties changed hands for £500 or less the cut-off point remained high in real terms.

In truth, the property qualification had not changed much in 150 years. Although in 1919 women were for the first time eligible for jury service, the character of the jury remained much the same; it had a stake in society and could be relied upon to continue to maintain the status quo. Few members of the working class were eligible for jury service, and the trade unions, after an initial burst of enthusiasm for overall representation on a jury, pursued the matter in a desultory fashion. Until 1949 there was no compensation for loss of wages. As Professor Cornish noted 'For the working man a jury summons could be an arduous financial burden'.[27] It is hardly surprising therefore that the unions did not actively press for more of their members to have the right to sit as jurors.

The next major development was brought about by rating revaluations in 1956 which, according to Lord Devlin, 'enabled a further one and a half million to become eligible for jury service, and subsequent revaluations by 1964 ensured that there was a pool of over seven million people available for jury service – 89% of whom were men'. The rating revaluations, followed by the enactment of the recommendations of the Morris Committee in 1972, changed the shape of criminal proceedings in this country. The Committee had recommended the abolition of the property qualification, suggesting instead that qualification would be citizenship.

Over the years there had, of course, been other changes. The special jury had fallen into disuse, as had the grand jury. The grand jury had faded away with the rise of the magistracy and the use of committal proceedings to determine whether there was a case for the defendant to answer before he was sent for trial by the common jury. The grand jury had had a long and venerable history. Latterly, its role was to determine whether or not the prosecution evidence amounted to a 'true bill'. For local dignitaries it was also a social occasion of the first water. But it was a cumbersome device and was abolished in 1933.

There was also a reduction in the number of peremptory challenges. Originally, in treason and grand felony cases, there had been 35 in number, probably to ensure that no member of the grand jury tried the case, but the 1949 Administration of Justice Act drastically reduced that number to seven.

Towards the end of the 1960s came the first radical change which was to begin the erosion of the criminal jury. The Criminal Justice Act 1967 abolished the requirement that there must be a unanimous decision. Now, after a deliberation of at least two hours, a verdict of not less than ten of the twelve members in favour of either a guilty verdict or an acquittal would suffice.

One problem resulting from these changes became apparent immediately after the property qualification had been removed. There was a startling change in the type of serving juror. With wives and single adults now eligible to sit the jury was no longer middle-aged, middle-class and white. (There is some evidence, however, that for many years there were disproportionately fewer jurors drawn from the ethnic minorities.) Even though today's system is still far from perfect the jurors of today are much closer to the concept of a random cross-section of society.

Even before the abolition of the property qualification the rating revaluations of the 1950s and 1960s meant that there were many more jurors who had encountered the police in very different circumstances to those of their predecessors a few years before. Jurors were less prepared to accept what the police said in a wholly uncritical manner. Whilst D.N.Pritt, writing as 'a Barrister', might have been pleased, others thought that the new jurors did not have the integrity or ability of the jurors who had served so well over the previous 150 years.

In evidence to the Morris Committee the Metropolitan Police Commissioner stated that after the rating revaluations 'there had been a marked deterioration in the quality of jurors'. The Commissioner was by no means alone in his view. Another commentator who submitted written evidence to the Committee suggested that 'there is an increasing number of men and women of poor education who are ill-equipped for such (jury) service ... the position may be expected to deteriorate still further'.[28]

There was also at about this time a 'jury nobbling' scare, something which crops up regularly in the history of the jury. In this instance though, there was never any evidence that the practice was widespread, or that any jury had succumbed to the nobblers; nevertheless, the seeds of suspicion were sown. A close watch was kept on juries over the next few months. It seems that nobbling was a London phenomenon amounting to some three cases of attempted jury interference noted by the Metropolitan Police.

As a result of these cases the Home Secretary requested Parliamentary assistance. There was no attempt made to explore any long-term preventive measures. Instead, after 600 years of unanimous verdicts the Criminal Justice Act 1967 introduced the concept of verdict by majority. The measure remains arguably the most controversial reform of the jury system this century.

The 1970s witnessed a number of remarkable developments in the jury system. First the Morris Committee's proposals to abolish the property qualification were adopted. Henceforth citizenship and not property would be the criterion for jury selection; a reform calculated to bring to bear on society's problems the 'corporate good sense of the community'.

Then in 1972, after the defence in the Angry Brigade trial success-fully persuaded the judge to question the jurors with a view to estab-lishing political bias, the following Practice Direction was issued to all judges:

A jury consists of twelve individuals chosen at random from the appropri-ate panel; a juror is excused if he is personally concerned in the facts of the case, or closely connected with a party to the proceedings or with a prospective witness. He may also be excused at the discretion of the judge on grounds of personal hardship or conscientious objection to jury service. It is contrary to established practice for jurors to be excused on more general grounds such as race, religion, political beliefs, or occupation.[29]

A further notable development in which the scope of the jury trial was diminished came in 1977 when the Criminal Law Act removed the right of trial by jury in such cases as causing criminal damage with a value of £100 or less (later increased to £400 and now to £2,000) and various public order offences. The practical implications were immediately apparent in the courts. 1977 was the year of the Grunwick dispute in which some 500 people were arrested, mainly for public order offences. Trial by jury was no longer available to them.

That same Act saw the right of the defence to use seven peremptory challenges reduced to three. The Crown retained its right of stand-by – the equivalent of a challenge with almost unlimited effect. It was a remarkable reform in view of the fact that within the year it became public knowledge that jury vetting was being routinely carried out by prosecutors in politically sensitive cases; the purpose of such vetting being to weed out those jurors whom the prosecution thought 'dis-loyal' or otherwise 'unsuitable'.

The Criminal Justice Act 1988 has brought further major changes to this area of the law. Under this statute the defence have now entirely lost the right of peremptory challenge. Also, the right to elect jury trial has been withdrawn for offences of driving whilst disqualified, common assault, and taking a motor vehicle without consent. And the minimum loss or damage in a case alleging criminal damage must now be at least £2,000 before a defendant can take his case before a jury. Finally, the Act also removes from the province of the jury issues of *autre fois* convict and *autre fois* acquit. These issues, which together go to make up the expression 'double jeopardy', will now be heard by a judge.

The purpose and effect of this trend will be considered in the chapters that follow, together with an assessment of the modern jury and some reforms which may be desirable. Before doing so, it will be useful to consider the delicate question of the relationship between State and jury.

Chapter 2

The State against the Jury

It is fair to say that generations of English-speaking people have been weened on Blackstone's notion that the jury is a 'bulwark of liberty'. Lord Devlin described the jury as 'a protection against tyranny' and 'the lamp that shows that freedom lives'.[1] He was expressing a view that has taken root in the public consciousness. Certainly the Morris Committee declared that there is 'a conviction in the minds of the public that a jury is in a very real sense a safeguard of our liberties'.[2]

There is now another, quite different view which has gained the broad acceptance of most academics. Professor Jackson, writing in what has become a standard students' textbook, had this to say: 'I should like to think that the idea of the jury as a safeguard of the liberty of the individual had been decently buried.' Also, on the subject of seditious libel trials: 'I have examined many of the late eighteenth century trials for seditious libel ... and for every acquittal there was a conviction to balance it.'[3]

Professor Jackson's view has come to represent the mainstream of academic opinion. It is shared in part at least by Professors Cornish and Glanville Williams. Professor Williams has this to say: 'Objective research does not show that juries were ever remarkable for acquitting in political cases against the weight of the evidence.' Also, '... the assumption that political liberty at the present day depends upon the institution of the jury ... is in truth merely folklore.'[4]

These views reflect a distinction that can be made between run-of-the-mill criminal trials where juries mitigated the effects of a harsh penal code with the tacit approval or even at the instigation of the trial judge, and trials that were essentially political, wherein lay the real area of conflict between judge and jury. And it is on this count that these criticisms are based.

The views of such eminent academics cannot be lightly dismissed. Indeed, there is some force in the criticisms to the extent that there have been many occasions when individual juries have failed to live up to the expectations of Lord Devlin. There are three criticisms that have been levelled at juries with some justification: failure to protect individuals; acting out of bias (most commonly class or religion); and an inability to prevent judges or prosecutors from extending the scope of the law unfairly.

Arguably, a case in which all three of these criticisms are represented is that of the Tolpuddle Martyrs. These six working men formed a Friendly Society. This was not an illegal act in itself, though their bloodthirsty oath to secrecy alarmed local landowners who cast around for a means of putting these upstarts in their place. A prosecution was launched under the Mutiny Act of 1797, an Act passed to stamp out naval mutinies by making it illegal for servicemen to administer oaths of secrecy to their comrades. Notable features of the trial were the inappropriateness of the charges, the reluctance of the prosecution witnesses, and the hostility of the judge to the defendants. The jury obediently convicted the six defendants who were each sentenced to seven years' transportation.

The case of the Tolpuddle six was a black mark in the history of the jury and it was not an isolated one by any means. These are unavoidable and disappointing conclusions, but it is still generally true that where the liberty of an individual is at stake his best hope for a just trial lies not with a magistrate or a judge but with a jury. This is so now as it has been for centuries.

We do not elevate juries to the kind of unqualified admiration offered by Blackstone or Lord Devlin but we do put forward two propositions for consideration. First, that the jury has played a much greater role in protecting the liberties of the individual than its critics would have us believe. These critics have failed to give sufficient weight to a crucial factor: that since the inception of jury trial in this country one of the enduring features of the criminal law has been a struggle for control over individual juries, by vetting, packing or other such malpractices, or simply by judicial threats, bribes or other forms of coercion. Criticisms of particular jury failures should be tempered, therefore, by the knowledge that these have often sprung from the application of one or more controls over the jury.

Second, the jury has contributed to the establishment of a just and humane system of criminal justice, and its presence continues to maintain this state of affairs. In the words of one senior prosecuting barrister 'I'm always aware of the jury looking over my shoulder, willing me to be fair.' In this role it can still provide a check against the occasional political prosecution. Perhaps this may prove to be the lasting lesson of the trial of Clive Ponting.

Clive Ponting was the senior Civil Servant tried on a charge under Section 2 of the Official Secrets Act for leaking classified documents to a Member of Parliament. Clive Ponting was to confirm in evidence at his trial what many suspected: that Government ministers had been lying to Parliament about the sinking of the Argentinian cruiser, the *General Belgrano*. It was argued on behalf of Mr Ponting that the statute allowed such disclosure if it was 'in the interests of state' and that his disclosure of information to Tam Dalyell MP came within this provision.

McCowan J. disagreed and directed the jury that 'the interests of state' should be equated with the interests of the political party in power. The summing up was all but a direction to convict. The acquittal of Clive Ponting demonstrated that the jury can still be a force to be reckoned with. It is refreshing that even specially vetted jurors will still follow the dictates of conscience.

It may be significant that the trial of Clive Ponting was the last major secrets trial of its kind in this country. There have been subsequent occasions when the Government has moved to suppress the dissemination of classified information. These include most notably the Zircon Affair and the Spycatcher and Cavendish memoirs. Significantly the Government has chosen to avoid criminal prosecutions (and therefore jury trial) and elected to seek injunctions in the High Court. It may be that we shall soon see a return to criminal prosecutions. Under the Official Secrets Act 1989 any leak by a Civil Servant is all but an offence of strict liability. The Government has made clear its determination to prevent any repetition of the Ponting acquittal.

It might be fair to say that the best measure of juries are the tactics developed by governments, judges, and prosecutors to secure convictions when faced with recalcitrant jurors. It is to these that we now turn.

Bypassing the jury

On reading histories of the troubled relationship between State and juries it is surprising that the jury system has survived at all. This may be due in part to the fact that the value of a jury verdict does not lie in a simple finding of fact – guilt or innocence – but in the stamp of legitimacy conferred by a decision shared by twelve independent citizens. This in itself probably accounts for the survival of an institution whose power has traditionally been both secured and coveted by the State. There have, however, been occasions in our history when the usual methods of coercing verdicts from juries have been deemed unreliable or inconvenient and the State has chosen to bypass jury trial. History provides us with many examples, often with modern parallels.

Bills of attainder

This draconian measure, involving a simple Act of Parliament denouncing an individual as a traitor, was usually employed against the King's enemies, particularly those who actually took part in open warfare against the Crown. It was also used by Parliament for purely political ends, for instance, to secure the death of the Earl of Wentworth in 1641 and that of Archbishop Laud (after an unsuccessful attempt to prosecute for treason) in 1645. A Bill of Attainder was employed in 1651 against John Lilburne, one of the most awkward political opponents of Cromwell's regime. The effect of the Act in Lilburne's case was merely to banish on pain of death. We have already noted in Chapter 1 that Lilburne returned to England two years later in breach of the act. He was prosecuted for being in England contrary to statute and acquitted by a jury.

Ex-officio informations

Ex-officio informations were the prerogative of the Attorney-General. They were much used in the eighteenth and early nineteenth centuries in relation to seditious libel trials. They were in effect a neat way of dispensing with grand juries and bringing cases directly before special juries who were amenable to the Crown.

The net result was to bypass an important safeguard for the defendant, for in its heyday the grand jury performed a number of functions which are now more efficiently, if more mundanely, dealt with by magistrates. Its prime role was that of throwing out untenable cases or returning a 'true Bill' thereby sending a case for trial before judge and jury. Unlike many special jurors, grand jurors were composed of local worthies, men of substance and independence. The use of this tactic in dubious political prosecutions gave an added advantage to the Crown.

Though the grand jury was abolished in 1933 in favour of modern committal proceedings there are still cases in which the prosecution will seek to avoid pre-trial proceedings, to gain a tactical advantage or to secure some financial saving at the expense of the rights of a defendant. The Voluntary Bill of Indictment is one such method of dispensing with pre-trial proceedings in the magistrates' court. In a recent case prosecution lawyers avoided the prospect of lengthy committal proceedings against the unrepresented Earnest Saunders. A delay was obtained to allow the provisions of the recent Criminal Justice Act (1988) to take effect. The provisions of the Act allow a 'transfer certificate' to take the place of committal proceedings.

Suspension of jury trial

So far as we can establish, this tactic was only ever adopted in the colonies, perhaps because what was possible to enact for the colonies would never have been tolerated in mainland Britain. Certainly, throughout the history of the jury, vetting and packing were never more enthusiastically pursued by the Crown than in Ireland.[5] There were occasions in the nineteenth century when even these measures were deemed to be insufficient: acquittals were said to be perverse and many jurors were thought to be liable to intimidation. Suspension of jury trial was the usual response. It has become a familiar scenario: the Diplock Courts (which we discuss in Chapter 8) have been in operation for 18 years without any indication of a return to jury trial.

Transferring cases to the magistrates' courts

Trial before the justices has always proved to be a safe option for the executive. The modern trend of transferring cases to the magistrates, or merely keeping cases before the magistrates, is a tactic that is discussed more fully in Chapter 6 but it is also necessary to touch upon this topic here.

One of the earliest instances in which this tactic was first employed was in relation to the game laws, which were perhaps the most despised body of laws on the statute books. Until the Game Act of 1831 the right to shoot game was confined to those possessing freehold property of at least £100 p.a. (in other words, gentlemen only). For the peasantry, taking game was more than sport, it was a modest supplement to income and diet. The savage enforcement of the game laws was an integral part of rural life. It was no coincidence that these laws were usually enforced by those for whose benefit they had been passed – the landed gentry sitting as justices. Sidney and Beatrice Webb wryly observed: 'It is characteristic of the English country gentleman that it was not to the love of money that their judicial impartiality and intellectual integrity succumbed but to their overmastering desire to maintain their field sports.'[6]

It is hardly surprising that cases coming before juries were frequently unsuccessful in the face of the most compelling evidence. Lord Kenyon's account of a trial over which he presided provides one example of dumb insolence by a jury. The defendant was charged with unlawfully shooting game, and the evidence was clear cut: 'the defendant's counsel was hard pressed. At length, "Gentlemen," said he, "it's true that they have shown my client fired at the bird, and that he bagged it. It is no use to deny that. But how does it appear that the bird was killed by the shot? What proof is there that it did not die of the fright?" The jury acquitted.'[7]

Less attractive has been the refusal of juries in the 1960s and 1970s to convict in drink-drive cases, exercising a 'there but for the grace of God go I' principle. Their behaviour has given rise to a change in the law and that in itself is a more modern example of the continuing struggle between the State and the jury. The right of defendants to elect trial in these sort of cases has simply been withdrawn. Setting aside arguments of expense to the public purse there is much to be said for jury trial as a means of educating citizenry.

One other such reform occasioned by the Criminal Law Act of 1977 rendered a number of public order offences triable only before magistrates. This was the summer of the Grunwick dispute when some 500 people were arrested and tried on charges which no longer carried the opportunity of seeking jury trial. These cases were heard by justices and stipendiary magistrates. The prosecutions relied entirely on police evidence. Harman and Griffiths commented that: 'In the majority of cases the police evidence was so thin as to be derisory. Here was a factor which would have seriously concerned a jury but hardly seemed to matter to the magistrates.'[8]

The tactic of shifting the trial venue is nothing new, but lately the authorities have wrapped up decisions to deny the opportunity of jury trial on the altruistic grounds of economy and reducing pre-trial delays. This procedure is just another method by which the effects of a troublesome jury can be mitigated.

Fixing the trial venue

This was a tactic employed in Ireland often in a bid to bring the case before pro-Government juries. It was also used occasionally in England particularly in relation to prosecutions under the Black Act of 1723. This Act was directed against the practice of going 'blacked up' to take game in royal parks. E.P.Thompson records that many juries returned verdicts 'contrary to the evidence' and trials were transferred to the King's Bench, 'a less expensive method ... and rather more effectual; especially now we may depend upon having juries of men of probity and well enclined towards their King's and country's service and interest'.[9] In other words, 'well enclined' towards convicting in order that the status quo be maintained. 'Probity' in this context had strong political connotations.

Only a few years later we find that trials of Sussex smugglers were being transferred to Chichester, partly for the convenience of the witnesses (a legitimate concern), but also where 'a sheriff can get a petty jury whose probity can be depended upon'.[10]

The power to transfer trials is now rarely exercised and never abused. A transfer may be sought by the Crown or on behalf of the defendant, usually to avoid some perceived prejudice against the accused.[11]

Vetting

Although vetting and packing of jurors are closely related activities they ought to be distinguished, although it is true to say that vetting in the past was usually simply a necessary prelude to packing. Vetting is concerned only with checking out background information on jurors. Jury vetting was a logical development of a system which allowed parties to a trial the scope to influence jury composition through challenging. In practice only the Crown had the resources to carry out systematic vetting, and when the case came to trial the prosecution's right to stand-by until the panel was exhausted far outweighed the defendant's rights of challenge.

Vetting by the Crown allied to heavy use of the stand-by was particularly marked in the treason and seditious libel trials of the eighteenth century. Surviving Treasury Solicitor's papers show the extent and thoroughness of the vetting operation. E. P. Thompson records that 'On one such list the names from which the jury were to be drawn were marked G (good), B (bad) and D (doubtful)'.[12]

The prosecution of William Hone in 1817 for seditious and blasphemous libel provides an example. Preparations by the Crown were thorough. Requests for information about potential special jurors were sent out and some of the replies still lie in the papers of the Treasury Solicitor. Here is one example:

> My Dear Sir,
> Most willingly and most heartily would I do what you require if I could, but I cannot point out any general quarter of information. I should think Rivington's might give useful information. One better than Joshua Watson you could not have selected, of individual persons you could not have two better than John Patterson of Old Broad Street and Jon Sotton of St Helen's Place. John Gibson is a capital juryman in civil matters but he is a Presbyterian or rather a Unitarian.[13]

Vetting on this scale coupled with a robust use of the stand-by served to weed out most jurors who might not be sympathetic to the Government. Perhaps these factors go some way to explaining Professor Jackson's observation of seditious libel trials of this period that 'for every acquittal there was a conviction to balance it'.

The practice of vetting continues to flourish, though what was once done by the Treasury Solicitor is now the preserve of the Special Branch and a department of M.I.5. This is a subject we examine in Chapter 3 in greater detail.

Packing

Packing was once commonplace. It was almost a feature of local politics. Local histories are thick with accounts of the gentry who 'drummed up indictments and used packed juries against each other'.[14] Much more objectionable was the use of jury packing against defendants in run-of-the-mill criminal trials or those who had perhaps inadvertently fallen foul of some man of influence or some aspect of Government policy.

Perhaps one of the earliest references to jury packing appears in the trial of Sir Nicholas Throckmorton for treason in 1554. Throckmorton is recorded as having interrupted judge and prosecutor as they discuss the composition of the jury. We do not know exactly what was being said, but Throckmorton's comment is plain enough: 'Will this foul packing never cease?'[15] This was a comment echoed by John Lilburne in 1649 who demanded to be tried by a court that was not 'special, prejudged, packed ...'[16] And again, nearly 250 years later, by Lord Hutchinson in the trial of Aubrey, Berry, and Campbell in 1978. Another example is the case of the jurors empanelled to try Thomas Hardy in 1794, who were described by a contemporary observer as 'a most extraordinary assemblage, King's tradesmen, contractors, and persons labouring under every kind of bias and influence'.[17]

Special juries, drawn largely from the ranks of the higher social classes could generally be depended upon. Special juries could try only misdemeanours and as such one of their most notable functions was that of trying seditious and blasphemous libel cases, particularly in the eighteenth and nineteenth centuries.

One such case involved William Hone (1817). Hone published three political parodies which mocked the corruption in Government. Charges of seditious and blasphemous libel were soon laid. At each of his trials Hone entertained jurors with an account of how they (the jurors) had been chosen to sit on the trial. He told them of the meeting before the 'Master' to strike the jury panel. The method used by the Master was to let his pen fall at random on the pages of the jury book. It was a rough and ready method which might have worked well but for the fact that the names called out by the master were not those indicated by his pen. At his first trial, Judge Abott tried to prevent this flow of embarrassing information but was restrained by, of all people, a juror.

It may well be that this tactic helped secure Hone's acquittal on all charges. Certainly this was a tactic that was well tested; it was used with success by Horne Tooke at his trial for seditious libel in 1777, and nearly two hundred years later it was to be employed to good effect by Platts Mills QC during the trial of some alleged gunrunners. One can only speculate as to what Horne Tooke's jury made of his account of how the jury panel had been rigged:

The first name that I took notice of was Mr Sainsbury, a tobacconist on Ludgate Hill. The Sheriff's officer said, he had been dead seven months; that struck me. I am a snuff taker, and buy my snuff at his shop, therefore I knew Mr Sainsbury was not so long dead. I asked him strictly if he was sure Mr Sainsbury was dead, and how long had he been dead. 'Six or seven months.' Why I read his name today, he must then be dead within a day or two. For I saw in the newspapers that Mr Sainsbury was appointed by the City of London ... to receive the toll of the Thames navigation, and as the City of London does not often appoint dead men for these purposes, I concluded that the Sheriff's officer was mistaken, and Mr Sainsbury was permitted to be put down amongst you, Gentlemen, appointed for this special jury.[18]

Packing in Ireland was slightly more extreme. Throughout the eighteenth and nineteenth centuries vetting by the Crown was supplemented by an aggressive use of the stand-by. The effect was to produce what became known as 'castle juries' – a pointed reference to Dublin Castle, seat of British rule in Ireland. The practice brought about some particularly unjust results in a country racked by land disputes between the native Catholic Irish and the mainly Protestant British settlers. John McEldowney cites a contemporary description of one such trial: 'Twenty-five jurors in all were asked to stand aside, all but three being Catholic and the result was eleven Protestants and one Catholic, a landlord, to try an Irish peasant.'[19]

Perhaps the most blatant episode of packing arose out of the trial of one McKenna. The background to this trial must be monotonously familiar to any student of Irish history. McKenna was a Catholic, charged with the murder of a Protestant during factional disturbances in Monaghan. The defence, led by Isaac Butt, successfully challenged the array on the grounds that the under sheriff had deliberately summonsed a jury panel which was of an overwhelmingly Protestant/settler background.[20] McKenna later stood his trial elsewhere and was acquitted.

The practice of institutionalised jury packing would seem to be a thing of the past. In recent years, however, there have been instances of trial lawyers complaining in fairly forceful terms that the composition of a particular jury must be an unhappy coincidence or something more sinister.

One such trial became known as the Welsh Language trial (1978). Two radical members of the Welsh Language Society were tried at Carmarthen on a charge of conspiracy to damage a radio transmitter. This, the prosecution alleged, was part of their campaign for a Welsh television channel. Despite the fact that Carmarthen was one of the stronger Welsh-speaking areas of Wales, only one of the jurors was able to follow the evidence of the defendants (which was in Welsh). Eleven of the jurors had English surnames. At the time the striking dissimilarity between the social composition of the jury and the catchment area from which is was drawn attained the status of a minor legal scandal. It seems probable that the introduction of jury selection by the application of random numbers to the electoral role has finally laid such grievances to rest.

Bribery and corruption

Corruption of jurors is a recurring theme in the history of the jury system, mainly, it seems, by persuasion or intimidation. There is no evidence that it was ever widespread or organised until the last few years, when senior officers of the Metropolitan Police alleged that there was at least one jury nobbling gang at work in the London area. We deal with this issue in more detail in Chapter 10.

Bribery was an option open to all, at least to those who had the means. Treasury Solicitors tended to draw the line at this point, they were deterred perhaps by a belated sense of scruples or, more probably, parsimony and a tendency to rely on other, cheaper, techniques of jury control.

There was one exception - the 'guineamen'. These individuals made up the numbers on special juries. As their name suggests, they received a guinea for every trial they sat on. Their retention on the lists of guineamen depended on them returning verdicts acceptable to the Crown. Jeremy Bentham recalls that until the mid-eighteenth century guineamen were paid two guineas for a conviction and one for an acquittal.[21]

An example of bribery and corruption in action is given by E. P. Thompson in his description of the preparations of Baptist Nunn for the Special Commission at Reading in 1723: 'drumming up evidence, suborning witnesses, alternatively bribing and threatening the prisoners'. Not content with this, arrangements were made to rig the jury panel. Baptist Nunn's expense sheets still exist to tell the tale: 'altering pannell £1', and 'To Windsor with some of the jury ... £1 ...'[22]

Judicial bias and state intimidation

Judicial bias was once so common as to be unremarkable. Perhaps the best known of this breed of judge were Braxfield, who presided over the Scottish treason trials of the 1790s, and Judge Jeffreys of the Bloody Assizes.

An early and extreme example is recorded by Bellamy. It arose out of the trial of a number of friars for treason in 1402. The jury convicted the defendants but 'after the execution its members came weeping to those friars who were collecting the corpses. They explained that unless they returned a verdict of guilty they would have been put to death themselves.'[23]

This last case in which physical force was threatened would seem to have been an isolated example, though Bentham records one case where the jurors were in some doubt. One of the jurors was called forward 'and he was set upon the clerks' table, and the judge and he whispered together a great while; and it was observed that the judge having his hands upon his shoulders would frequently shake him as he spoke to him'.[24]

When these methods were not sufficient the fining and imprisoning of juries was one method of indicating judicial displeasure at verdicts which did not follow the judge's direction. Examples of this include the jurors who acquitted Throckmorton (1554) and Penn and Mead (1670). The trial of Penn and Mead gave rise to Bushell's case in which the principle of verdict according to conscience was established. This did not mean, however, that thereafter jurors were free from judicial pressure. Bullying and cajoling verdicts from juries was common until well into the nineteenth century.

Judicial bias is still a feature of our trial system. We deal with this phenomenon more fully in Chapter 10. It is only necessary at this stage to point out that during the summer of 1988 there was a spate of cases in which convictions were set aside by the Court of Appeal on the grounds of bias by the trial judge.[25]

Refusing to accept verdicts

The device of refusing to accept a verdict often involved directing a jury to reconsider its decision. Occasionally it went further and acquitted defendants were taken back into custody on the grounds that 'it is possible that other indictments may be laid'.[26]

Perhaps the only modern instance of such behaviour arose out of a murder trial at the Old Bailey in 1987. William Jennings was charged with the murder of his brother. He had been drinking and was involved in a scuffle with a third man during which he had

33

brandished a knife. Jennings' brother intervened and was fatally stabbed through the heart. Jennings pleaded not guilty to murder but during the course of the trial tendered a plea to manslaughter. The evidence indicated a tragic accident and the defendant was clearly distraught. Both prosecution and trial judge agreed to a plea to the lesser charge which would avoid the mandatory life sentence. It was perhaps a classic example of counsel misreading a jury. When asked to go through the formality of recording a verdict of not guilty to murder and guilty to manslaughter the jury refused to convict.

There then followed a scene worthy of the best traditions of the jury. 'Every one of us is saying he is not guilty. However long you make us stay here, it is still not guilty,' said one intrepid juror. The jury was sent out to reconsider its position no less than three times, each time remaining unmoved. The trial judge then took the unprecedented step of discharging the jury and proceeding straight to sentence. It may be that the jurors had a better understanding of their customary rights than the judge cared to admit. If this precedent is followed and extended then there will soon be no need for a jury at all.

Special verdicts

This was another device designed to secure convictions, used mainly in seditious libel trials. The trial judge would direct the jury to decide only whether the defendant published the work in question. This simple fact was rarely in dispute, the sting in the tail was that the judge would reserve to himself the real question as to whether the material was seditious, with predictable results. Where this ruling was applied it reduced the jury to a rubber stamp.

Not surprisingly convictions followed, though there were a sufficient number of acquittals to keep this scandal in the public eye. The trial of Henry Woodfall was one such case. In 1752 Woodfall was indicted for seditious libel for publishing material which was critical of the administration. The verdict of the jury was 'guilty of publishing only' which effectively amounted to an acquittal. It was a verdict which was to be echoed in a series of cases culminating in the trial of the Dean of St Asaph for publishing a pamphlet ('A dialogue between a Gentleman and a Farmer') advocating some fairly unexceptional Parliamentary reforms. The scandal which ensued led directly to the passing of Foxe's Libel Act, which declared that it was for the jury 'to give their verdict on the whole matter in issue.'

Conclusions

It is undeniably the case that juries have held out a real measure of protection for the liberties of the individual. This is so despite a history disfigured by every conceivable abuse and pressure to undermine the independence of individual juries. One cannot argue sensibly that because the juries have sometimes faltered in the face of these pressures the institution is therefore without merit and ought to be abolished. As always it is worth asking, what were the alternatives? There never was one.

In the seventeenth century juries offered the only real protection to Quakers prosecuted under the Conventicles Act for practising their religion. There were many acquittals against the evidence. In this sense the cases of Penn and Mead and that of Bushell have been attributed an importance that is theirs by chance. The fining and imprisonment of jurors was so common as to be unexceptional. It was also a political scandal and it is clear that the independence of the jury was won by a sustained conflict between individual jurors and the judges. The independence of juries became simply a question of time, a battle won by their own efforts. The Penn and Mead trial was typical of the trials of this period, although the characters were perhaps slightly larger than life, the issues in sharper relief. The defendants were more eloquent, the judge more biased, more vindictive in defeat, and the jury more obdurate in the face of adversity.[27]

As to the eighteenth century, to count up the verdicts in seditious and blasphemous libel trials and to conclude that 'for every acquittal there was a conviction to balance it' is simply to misunderstand the extent of interference with juries and the effect of acquittals. E. P. Thompson has suggested that the acquittals of Hardy, Thelwall, and Tooke, on charges of treason may have prevented a purge similar to the Red Terror taking place in France. Hardy's information was that: 'no fewer than 800 warrants against reformers had been drawn up ... which were to be served immediately upon a verdict being obtained against him'.[28]

It has been pointed out by the critics of the jury that as the nineteenth century progressed juries became more conservative and even reactionary. This would appear to be correct, perhaps as a response to events in France. It is also arguable that the movement for radical political reform was thwarted by the modest reforms that were made. The Juries Act of 1825 and the Reform Act of 1832 gave those who might otherwise have been the most vocal reformers a stake in society. As a result, partly by accident and partly by design, the jury became a bulwark of the status quo. The difference between the new juryman and his predecessors is almost intangible, not only new found prosperity but also an awkward class consciousness and jealousy of his new position.

Nevertheless, juries continued to contribute to the shape of the criminal law. The practice of 'pious perjury' continued to force the legislators to find alternatives to capital punishment. One classic example of juries making law may be found in their treatment of cases of infanticide.

Infanticide was a major social problem but the letter of the law was crude and inflexible; it was treated as a species of murder and therefore punishable by death. Malcolmson notes that serving maids were frequently defendants in such trials and eloquently explains their vulnerability: 'The frustrations of their confinement, the frequent and close contact with manservants, their subordinate and ambiguous relationship with the master and any mature sons he might have. . . . '[29] Pregnant and unmarried, the discovery of her condition would very likely result in the maid being turned out of the household. This was a common reason for the offence of infanticide.

Not infrequently juries ignored their oath and returned verdicts of acquittal. Where convictions were obtained they were often accompanied by mercy riders. Inevitably, the law was forced to change, first through the practice of commuting death sentences, and then finally in 1922 Parliament approached the problem by the creation of a non-capital offence under the Infanticide Act.

A degree of conflict between State and jury continues, arguably an inevitable and healthy feature of our society. In recent years the conflict has centred around freedom of speech, in particular the dividing line between art and obscenity. Penguin Books were unsuccessfully prosecuted in 1960 for publishing *Lady Chatterley's Lover*. A jury found *Inside Linda Lovelace* ('true story of a porn star') to be obscene but so too was *Last Exit to Brooklyn*, a book of some literary merit.

In 1976 a jury was prepared to lay down limits to permissiveness. An edition of *Gay News* published a poem ('The love that dare not speak its name') which suggested that after his crucifixion Christ had been sodomised by a centurian and that he himself had engaged in homosexual acts during his lifetime. The jury convicted both editor and magazine of blasphemous libel. In 1989 the proprietor of an art gallery who exhibited in his display a human foetus was convicted on a charge of causing a public mischief.

It is difficult to point to any consistent principles underlying any of these verdicts. But magistrates have fared little better; in some parts of the country ordering videos to be destroyed on the grounds of obscenity whereas elsewhere the same footage survives the scrutiny of the justices. All one can say is that juries possess two qualifications for this task in that they are independent and broadly representative of the community.

Much more contentious were the prosecutions of pacifists and members of the 'Troops Out' movement in the 1970s. There were some convictions for the distribution of leaflets to soldiers suggesting that they desert or outlining how they might buy themselves out of the army. In 1975 14 members of the 'British Withdrawal from Northern Ireland Campaign' were prosecuted at the Old Bailey for distributing such leaflets. This show trial, sanctioned at the highest Government levels, ended in embarrassing defeat for the authorities.

In the sphere of official secrets there have been a number of notable trials. Professor Jackson has cited one such case as an example of the spinelessness of jurors. In 1963 a number of nuclear disarmers, who organised a demonstration at an airbase, were charged with a breach of the Official Secrets Act and convicted by a jury. On the other hand, in 1970, Jonathan Aitken, then a journalist, was prosecuted for publishing classified Government information relating to the Nigerian civil war. The published material was embarrassing to the government. The jury, perhaps unimpressed by the motives behind the prosecution, acquitted. Much more recently of course, there was the acquittal of Clive Ponting in similar circumstances.

Before turning to consider jury vetting, one of the remaining devices of jury control, it is necessary to recognise that the main battle now is to ensure that in future the jury is not bypassed or abolished altogether. If we were ever to have a Bill of Rights jury trial ought to be high on the list for inclusion.

Chapter 3

Vetting

Jury vetting refers to the practice of carrying out checks on the backgrounds of jurors. We have already touched upon the nature and history of vetting in Chapter 2. In the United Kingdom vetting is only carried out by the Crown. Such checks are carried out for a number of reasons, most commonly to identify individuals who may be disqualified from jury service but also to identify those jurors who may be biased or unsympathetic to the Crown. It now seems clear that this involves not merely checks on criminal convictions but may also mean vetting by the Special Branch and M.I.5. In recent years the peculiarly secretive nature of this practice, with all its strong historical associations with jury packing, have given rise to considerable disquiet.

In this chapter we attempt to put the subject in perspective and assess its influence on the trial system. We also suggest some reforms. It might be appropriate to begin by examining the latest developments occasioned by the recent trial of Michael Bettaney on a charge of espionage.

Bettaney was an M.I.5 officer who had been passing classified information to Russian diplomats. After being caught and whilst he was awaiting trial in custody at Brixton prison he wrote to a Member of Parliament (the letter is set out in Appendix 1) outlining current jury vetting practices in relation to Official Secrets trials. The revelations of a spy might not ordinarily be given much weight so it is as well to point out that much of what Bettaney said was recently confirmed by the Attorney-General, and so far as we can judge none of what he said has been denied.[1] Bettaney had this to say of vetting: 'This process with which I am professionally familiar, involves record checks to establish whether a juror is a member of or sympathetic to any subversive party or organisation.' It seems that the list of subversives includes extreme members of the Labour Party or 'involvement in the peace movement or in industrial militancy'. This raises some interesting questions: Does the category of 'subversive' extend to active trade unionists? What criteria would be used to decide whether a Labour Party member was so extreme as to be excluded from jury service? Does the category of subversive apply also to the Greens and other political parties of that ilk? Why is there apparently no safeguard against extreme right wing bias?

Bettaney continued: 'These checks are supplemented by "in depth" discreet enquiries by the Special Branch amongst a person's colleagues, workmates, neighbours, and friends with a view to compiling a complete dossier on the person's political and social activities, his standing in the community and so forth.'

A number of observations arise. The activities described by Bettaney were in clear breach of the existing Attorney-General's guidelines. When jury vetting guidelines were first published on 11 October, 1978 the Attorney-General stated that: 'there is no question of telephone intercepts or the institution of inquiries by way of surveillance or otherwise, into occupations, family backgrounds, associates, political views and activities'.

On February 3, 1986 the Attorney-General was at pains to inform Parliament that this extraordinary contradiction was nothing more than a misunderstanding, 'inadvertently created'. This interpretation is not supported by a reading of the guidelines then in force nor is it supported by any contemporary evidence. The explanation smacks of *ex post facto* rationalisation and a concealment of systematic breaching of previous guidelines by the security services.

Secondly, Bettaney's assertion that vetting was a process with which he was 'professionally familiar' suggests that M.I.5 has played a much deeper role in jury vetting than has previously been admitted by the Government. This much has certainly been accepted by the Attorney-General.

The history of jury vetting is a strange one. Until recently it was thought to be of historical interest only. Although in one form or another it had been extant since the inception of the jury system it was thought to have died out in the nineteenth century. This was not correct; there is some evidence that in capital cases a certain amount of vetting continued to take place to ensure that abolitionists who might refuse out of conscience to return a guilty verdict were excluded from the jury panel.[2] C.H.Rolph revealed recently that the police were routinely and clandestinely engaged in vetting during the 1930s.[3] And if it is thought that these were isolated and perhaps limited instances this again is not correct. It may be that modern vettors can trace an unbroken lineage back to the days of Horne Tooke and William Hone.

Vetting remained a rather well-kept secret until the mid-1970s. It is indicative of its status that the details had to be wrung from unwilling law officers. It is fair to say in mitigation that an examination of Parliamentary exchanges up to 1975 makes it abundantly clear that senior law officers of successive administrations were unaware of what was being done in their names.[4]

There had been straws in the wind, of course,[5] but the first positive proof that vetting was still being practised by the Crown arose out of an IRA gun-running case at the Old Bailey in 1972. The prosecution 'stood-by' a number of jurors. As is usual when the stand-by is used, no reasons were given. The defence was led by John Platts Mills QC. His cross-examination of one Special Branch officer produced an interesting exchange, recorded for posterity by Geoffrey Robertson. A short extract will suffice:

Officer: 'There was written information from records against a number of names of the jurors. Information from Special Branch and other police records ...'

Platts Mills: 'Your objection has nothing to do with politics?'

Officer: 'I didn't say nothing to do with politics. The word "object" that I put against these jurors signified doubt about their political activities and their criminal activities.'[6]

The existence of vetting was by this time becoming increasingly hard to ignore; apparently respectable jurors were almost daily being stood-by without reason. Also the subject was being openly discussed by sections of the criminal Bar and the alternative press, strange bedfellows, surely.

Public perception was changed totally in 1978 during the so-called ABC trial. Crispin Aubrey and Duncan Campbell were investigative journalists who planned to write an article on British Signals Intelligence for *Time Out*. To that end they interviewed John Berry, a former corporal in Signals. Minutes after the interview they were all arrested by officers from the Special Branch on charges under the Official

Secrets Act 1911, sections 1 and 2. It seems that the flat had been bugged. The interview which was tape-recorded was later to form the basis of the prosecution case.

The trial of Aubrey, Berry, and Campbell, the ABC case, at the Old Bailey in the autumn of 1978 was remarkable for a number of reasons. It was the first time that the Official Secrets Act, section 1 (the spying clause), had been used against a journalist. Secondly, despite the Home Secretary's avowed intention to repeal this section of the Act the prosecution had been sanctioned by the Government's most senior officer, the Attorney-General; and, as such, the case epitomises the conflict in attitudes to secrecy in Government in this country. However, the lasting significance of what became known as the ABC trial lay in the public debate sparked off by revelations that not only had the Crown had the entire jury panel vetted but that vetting of panels had been going on for years, without the knowledge of defence lawyers.

A chance remark before the commencement of the trial made it apparent that the prosecution had obtained the jury panel list well before hand. The prosecution was forced to admit that a vet had taken place. Information had been extracted from the Criminal Records' Office, CID files, and from Special Branch with a view to having jurors, whom the prosecution thought to be 'unsuitable' or 'disloyal' to the State, stood-by. As Bettaney's letters indicate, it later transpired that there may also have been a degree of active spying on potential jurors by members of the Special Branch and M.I.5. The outcry occasioned by this surreptitious practice finally forced Attorney-General Sam Silkin to publish the Guidelines during the ABC trial in an effort to justify the practice. The Guidelines made their first public appearance in, of all places, *The Times*.

The rationale of jury vetting has remained constant. It was expressed by the Attorney-General in these terms: it was envisaged that in security cases where the evidence is to be heard in camera there is the danger of 'a juror making improper use of that evidence'. Also, 'potential jurors may be susceptible to improper pressure' or may, 'because of extreme political beliefs, be biased against the prosecution or defence'.[7] It ought to be said that only the Attorney-General has ever had the temerity to suggest that vetting was for the benefit of defendants. After all, it has now been established that the practice had been carried on by prosecutors regularly and in secret for years without the knowledge of defence lawyers.

The Guidelines were subsequently amended and reamended to take account of various court decisions and the fact that the police and security services were later found to have been breaching the Guidelines with impunity. The revised Guidelines represent considerable and hard-won refinements of earlier versions. The main provisions of the revised Guidelines are set out below together with recent Guidelines regulating the use of the stand-by. (The complete Guidelines as they appeared in 1988 are reproduced in Appendix 2 on pages 161–65.)

The Attorney-General's Guidelines on jury vetting

Under the latest Guidelines, vetting may only be carried out in terrorist cases or in security cases where some of the evidence is likely to be heard in camera. Vetting under these Guidelines requires the authority of the Attorney-General.

The methods by which jurors are to be vetted include (in any terrorist trial) record checks with the Criminal Records' Office and Special Branch. In security cases where evidence is likely to be heard in camera, then the security services 'may also be involved'; this extremely vague caveat was added as a result of the Bettaney revelations. No other checks may be made save to confirm the identity of a juror about whom checks are being made. The results of a vet will be sent to the Director of Public Prosecutions who will decide what information will be passed to prosecuting counsel.

The stand-by of jurors may only be exercised on the basis of such a vet with the consent of the Attorney-General. Before such a stand-by may be exercised there must be 'strong reason' to feel that 'a juror may be a security risk' or 'be susceptible to improper approaches'.

Where it seems that a juror may be biased against the accused, 'the nature and source' of the information permitting, the defence should be given an indication of why that juror might be biased. It has to be said that we have been able to trace only two instances in which the defence was given such an indication. Both of these instances arose only after the Guidelines had been published and when jury vetting had become firmly established as a national scandal. Also, as things stand, the abolition of the peremptory challenge renders this an empty concession. It seems clear that the prospects of making out a challenge for cause on the basis of such an indication are poor.

The Attorney-General's Guidelines on the use of the stand-by (see Appendix 2)

A few words about the use of the stand-by are necessary. The use of the stand-by has steadily declined from the heady days of the 1970s. A recent study of the use of the peremptory challenge carried out by the Crown Prosecution Service made an incidental finding that the prosecution stood-by one or more jurors in 5% of all trials studied.

The need for guidelines was occasioned by the abolition of the defence right of peremptory challenge in 1989. The Attorney-General then announced guidelines regulating the use of the stand-by. The use of the stand-by would, he said, be restricted to cases coming within the vetting guidelines or where a juror was 'manifestly unsuitable' and the defence agreed to the use of the stand-by in respect of such a juror.

Other forms of vetting

Vetting in ordinary criminal cases may be carried out to the extent that a check at the Criminal Records' Office may be made. This does not require the consent of the Director of Public Prosecutions or the Attorney-General. The Association of Chief Police Officers has indicated (see Appendix 2) that such vets will not be carried out save on the direction of the DPP or the Chief Constable in those cases in which (i) there is reason to believe that attempts are being made to circumvent the statutory provisions excluding disqualified persons from service on a jury, (ii) it is believed that in a previous related abortive trial an attempt was made to interfere with a juror or jurors, and (iii) in the opinion of the DPP or the Chief Constable it is particularly important to ensure that no disqualified person serves on the jury. Broadly speaking, no other vets are to be instigated save in accordance with the Attorney-General's Guidelines or to confirm the identity of a juror 'about whom the initial check has raised serious doubts'.

Arguments against vetting

Is vetting constitutional?
It is clearly desirable that individuals who are disqualified from jury service should not serve. Methods designed to achieve this aim are

largely uncontentious. There is, however, a strong argument that other forms of vetting are unconstitutional. In essence the argument is this: Parliament has laid down in the 1974 Juries Act the categories of individuals who are eligible for jury service. The same Act lays down the categories of those ineligible, excusable, or disqualified from jury service. If the classes of those who are disqualified from jury service are to be enlarged, this is a matter for Parliament and not the Attorney-General acting on an *ad hoc* basis.

In any case, Parliament has already legislated for the possibility of biased or corrupt jurors by introducing majority verdicts in 1967. In the same Act express provision was made to penalise jurors who might be sitting whilst disqualified. Again, if further safeguards are required to guard against biased, corrupt, or otherwise unsuitable jurors, then Parliament is the only body with the power to enact such reforms.

If these arguments need any reinforcement then one only need examine the law books of the period which reveal a rather odd state of affairs: a Royal Commission (the Morris Committee) had reported and a number of statutes culminating in the Juries Act 1974 had been passed, but nowhere is there to be found any reference to the practice of vetting. Effectively the prosecution has been ignoring the provisions set out in the Juries Act 1974 and the Lord Chief Justice's Practice Direction reaffirming the principle of random selection of jurors irrespective of 'race, religion, or political beliefs'.

Soon after the revelations in the ABC case the legal status of vetting was reviewed by the appellate courts, first by the Court of Appeal (Civil Division) in the Brownlow case, then only a few months later by the Court of Appeal (Criminal Division) in the Mason case. It is appropriate to consider how the courts have dealt with these issues.

In the case of *R. v. Sheffield Crown Court ex parte Brownlow* [1980] Q.B. 530, two police officers were indicted on charges of actual bodily harm. Their lawyers made an application to the trial judge for an order that the jury panel be vetted by the police on their behalf. Judge James Pickles granted the order and the Chief Constable appealed unsuccessfully to the Court of Appeal (Civil Division). The result turned on a legal point of jurisdiction and the case is relevant only because the judges involved commented in passing on the legality of vetting.[8]

Lord Denning was characteristically forthright on the subject: 'To my mind it is unconstitutional.' Shaw L.J. was equally blunt: 'Any order or direction of a court designed to facilitate the selection of a jury by methods not directly provided for by the Juries Act 1974 or recognised by the Common Law is unconstitutional.' Brandon L.J. was only a little more cautious: 'I have serious doubts whether there should be any vetting at all, either by the prosecution or the defence.'

A few months later the issue was once again before the courts. In June 1980 the Court of Appeal (Criminal Division) heard the case of *R. v. Mason* [1980] 71. Cr. App. R. 157. Mason's case is important not only because it is now the leading case on vetting but also because of the issues which were not decided at the time and remain unresolved to this day. Mason was convicted at Northampton Crown Court on two counts of burglary and two of handling stolen goods. He was sentenced to five years' imprisonment and applied for leave to appeal against his conviction on various grounds, in part because the jury which convicted him had been vetted in breach of the Attorney-General's Guidelines.

Certain facts were agreed for the purposes of the appeal: a Criminal Records' Office check had been carried out on the panel; four jurors had been asked to stand-by for the Crown; and the jury panel had been vetted in breach of the Attorney-General's Guidelines. Furthermore, as far as enquiries instigated by the Court could establish, at least one juror asked to stand-by was not disqualified by the Juries Act. Ten out of 100 jurors on the panel apparently had criminal records, but in six of these cases no positive link was established beyond a similarity of names. In a further two cases the convictions were for motoring offences. Out of the panel of 100 two were found to be disqualified.

Lawton L.J. read the judgement of the Court which ruled that 'The practice of supplying prosecuting counsel with information about potential jurors' convictions was not unlawful.' The Court ruled also that the supply of information relating to convictions which were not sufficient to disqualify a juror was legal.

At first sight Mason's case was an outright victory for the vettors; but a closer examination shows the case left the central issue undecided. This was primarily because the Court's jurisdiction was constrained by the Criminal Appeal Act 1968, Section 2(1) under which the appeal was launched. Mason's appeal relied on one limb of the section that the vetting amounted to a 'material irregularity in the course of the trial'. Since vetting took place before the trial it had to be conceded that it was beyond the jurisdiction of the Court. A fine legal distinction perhaps, but one which effectively put paid to Mason's prospects of a successful appeal on this point.

It also put paid to any chance of a fuller ruling on vetting. The only issue as to its legality which remained within the Court's jurisdiction was the use which the prosecution made of the information supplied after the defendant entered his plea, i.e. in the course of the trial. In this respect there was overwhelming authority for the use of the stand-by for the Crown. This line of logic, impeccable in its reasoning, deprived Mason of the opportunity for developing a coherent argument against vetting. In the context of the Court of Appeal's narrow terms of reference, the 1974 Act which laid down the categories of persons qualified to sit, and those disqualified, ineligible, and excusable was largely irrelevant.

Perhaps the most significant feature of the Mason case is that it did not decide whether the supply of information to prosecuting counsel, other than criminal convictions, was lawful. Lawton L.J. was careful to draw a distinction between the supply of information relating to previous convictions and the provision of other information to prosecuting counsel. In respect of the latter Lawton said 'We have not been concerned in any way with, and make no comment upon, the giving to prosecution counsel of information other than that relating to convictions, or with the desirability of making enquiries about members of a jury panel.'

To sum up, the Court of Appeal has legitimised vetting to the extent that the prosecution may unearth criminal convictions with a view to weeding out disqualified jurors together with those jurors whose criminal records may not actually disqualify but suggest that they may be biased. It remains a moot point whether any other vetting may be carried out. Regrettably, experience shows that information from the vet usually includes information which has no relevance to the issue of whether or not jurors are qualified to sit.

Fairness

Any information about jurors obtained through vetting is of use to an advocate irrespective of whether he appears for the Crown or for the defence. It is therefore fundamentally unfair that information should be supplied to the prosecution to which the defence is denied access. In the context of the ABC trial the effect was quite startling; it came to light in the course of the trial that the juror chosen to be foreman was a former member of the SAS. It seems highly likely that the prosecution was aware of this and only too happy to have such a juror sit on the trial. The defence, of course, would have been unaware of the background of any juror when exercising its challenges.

Another example was the case of the Shrewsbury pickets who were tried in the autumn of 1973 following incidents arising out of an industrial dispute. The prosecution stood-by six potential jurors who it later transpired were skilled labourers. Setting aside for a moment the issue of even-handedness between prosecution and defence there is another important issue. What criteria were used by the prosecution in standing-by these jurors? It seems likely that the sole criterion was that they had in common with the defendants a shared occupation. It is perhaps stretching the long arm of coincidence to suggest that they were all 'subversives', closet communists, or militant trade unionists. There is no reason in principle why that jury should not have contained one or more trade unionists. Arguably, in this case the use of vetting in conjunction with the stand-by was directed not to producing an unbiased jury but a degree of pro-conviction bias.

One other example arose out of the trial of 14 pacifists at the Old Bailey in 1975. The 14 faced charges under the Incitement to Disaffection Act. It was alleged they had been distributing pacifist literature to soldiers with a view to persuading them to desert. A number of the defendants chose to represent themselves, and though they used their challenges vigorously they had no information about the potential jurors, relying instead on luck and instinct. The prosecution was content to stand-by four jurors. Information from the vet meant that the effect of the stand-by had a potentially dramatic twofold impact. Firstly, by excluding those jurors that the prosecution thought unsuitable and secondly, by ensuring that the jurors who remained were made of the right stuff. In fact this specially vetted jury acquitted all 14 defendants.

Another equally disturbing aspect of vetting was pointed out by Professor Freeman.[9] For many years, *Archbold,* the advocate's Bible on criminal law and practice, contained misleading information. It is fundamental to a fair trial that the defence lawyers are conversant with, or at least have access to, the rules under which the trial is to be conducted. The notion that the prosecuting counsel only be privy to secret Government guidelines adds a distinctly Orwellian touch. Such an idea is hardly in accord with the fundamental maxim that 'Justice must not only be done but manifestly and undoubtedly be seen to be done.'[10]

The guidelines themselves inadvertently identify a further criticism of vetting, stating as they do that only 'certain exceptional types of cases of public importance' are to be vetted. These cases tend to relate to defendants whom the Government perceives as a threat to the State itself. They involve cases alleging terrorism, spying, or other breaches of the Official Secrets Act. (The Ponting trial is a classic example.) It is, in short, a category of cases which Government most wishes to be prosecuted successfully. This is one of the most disturbing features of vetting because it is precisely in that class of case, where the State is both prosecutor and alleged victim, that it should refrain from attempting to influence the composition of the jury. Whether, as in the eighteenth and nineteenth centuries, this is done by the use of the special jury, or by unpublished 'administrative guidelines', it amounts to much the same thing: stacking the odds in favour of a conviction.

If fairness means anything in criminal trials it means even-handedness. But whilst the prosecution has apparent ease of access to juror lists a minor scandal arose in 1987 when it was discovered that some solicitors were actually exercising the right to inspect the jury panel. This led to fears that some solicitors were facilitating jury nobbling. The actual number of inspections is, however, small. Several of London's major firms of criminal solicitors indicated that they had never undertaken this task and would decline to do so if asked by a client.[11]

A further criticism relates to consistency; within a matter of weeks of the guidelines being published, the Lord Advocate, speaking from the Government front benches, indicated that jury vetting was not carried out in Scotland and that there was no likelihood of its introduction.[12] It is rather odd that vetting can be justified for one part of Britain but not another.

Breach and enforcement

Since the guidelines do not have the force of law there are no sanctions for breach; nor are there any methods of overseeing their implementation. The Bettaney revelations are not the first time that a breach of the Guidelines has inadvertently come to light. Throughout 1979/80 it became increasingly obvious that that police forces in Northamptonshire, Pembrokeshire, and elsewhere were routinely vetting in all criminal cases in clear breach of the existing guidelines. Other police forces were more circumspect, although it was clear that in many cases low-ranking officers were carrying out vets on their own initiative.

It is not fanciful to suggest that at some stage in the future it will again be discovered that the guidelines are being flaunted regularly. It is equally probable that once the fuss over the abolition of the peremptory challenge has died down, the scope of the guidelines will be extended on some pretext or other.

Privacy

One of the inevitable consequences of the grudging disclosures of jury vetting was the engendering of a degree of suspicion and distrust of the law in equal proportions. The Persons Unknown case is a good example. This concerned six defendants who were tried before Judge Alan King Hamilton at the Old Bailey in the autumn of 1979. They were charged with unlawful possession of weapons and explosives and conspiracy to rob. It was alleged by the prosecution that the defendants were anarchists who sought to commit acts of violence to further their political ends. The case, it was said, involved 'strong political motives' and the prosecution successfully sought leave to vet the jury panel.

One has to feel sorry for the jurors who were called to sit on this trial. Not only was the prosecution vetting the panel, so also was the defence. The prosecution vet relied primarily on record checks with the security services, though it seems also that the Special Branch (and possibly M.I.5) had to do an amount of 'leg-work' checking on jurors' backgrounds. Perhaps their paths crossed that of the defence team.

Legal aid had been extended to the defence in order to carry out its own vet, on the basis that fairness demanded an even-handed approach. Approximately £5,000 of public money was spent by the defence on hiring private investigators before the mounting cost led to the withdrawal of legal aid for this particular aspect of the case. Thereafter the prosecution agreed to make available to the defence a limited amount of information which had been uncovered from its sources. The defence lawyers declined this offer, albeit belatedly, stating that vetting on behalf of the defence legitimised an indefensible practice. These scruples do not necessarily appeal to all lawyers, some of whom would argue that the interests of the client currently on trial are paramount.

The trial began sensationally. On the first day David Leigh of *The Guardian* published an article detailing information on jurors uncovered by the prosecution vet.[13] The following entries appeared against jurors' names:

Randolf, P. : address believed to be a squat;
Jean, R. : Once made a complaint against the police which was withdrawn;
Marion O. : Burgled;
Geraldine Y. : Victim of GBH [Grievous bodily harm];
Peter P. : car stolen by employee;
Albert S. : car broken into eight years previously;
Olwen P. : £700 stolen from handbag;
Sharon D. : associated with criminal;
Rosemary J. : son spent six months in a detention centre.

A total of eight jurors were found to have convictions, six of which were spent under the provisions of the Rehabilitation of Offenders Act 1974. A single juror possibly was disqualified; the Criminal Records' Office check was inconclusive. Much of the information had no relevance to the question of whether the jurors were qualified to sit.

As a result of this article the jury was discharged in favour of a freshly vetted panel. In the wider context the revelations stirred up a fresh debate and brought the practice finally and irrevocably into disrepute. The vet failed to identify with certainty even a single disqualified juror. The security services had pooled the collective technological resources of the State and had come up with little more than gossip.

Immediately after the trial ended, *Time Out* published the results of the abortive defence vet.[14] This included credit-rating checks on jurors, County Court debt decisions, and hire-purchase arrangements. Employment records also came under scrutiny, as did the life-styles of jurors. One juror was said to occupy 'a slum property in an Indian ghetto'. Another was said to share a house with 'one or more whores who trade off the premises, a croupier, and occasional transient deviants'. Another juror lived in a block of flats also occupied by 'one or two prostitutes'. The wife of one juror was described as 'cockney and brassy', whilst another had an 'acerbic middle-aged wife'. One juror was described as 'self-important', another as 'common'.

Not surprisingly, it was felt in many quarters that vetting was an unwarrantable intrusion into personal privacy; whilst the opinion of the man in the street is not greatly valued by those who administer the law it must at least be of significance in this instance, because the proper administration of justice in the country depends on the trust and respect of the individual. In particular, it rests on the willingness of individuals to contribute as jurors and witnesses in criminal trials. For many people it is the only contact they will ever have with the criminal courts, involving considerable inconvenience and even sacrifice. For a juror it may involve making difficult decisions which will have a profound effect on the lives of others. In this context very pressing reasons are needed to justify the covert investigation of jurors.

Conclusions

Useful distinctions can be made between vetting in order to weed out disqualified and ineligible jurors and other forms of vetting designed to unearth possible bias or potential security risks among jurors.

Mason's case makes it clear that we require a more effective mechanism for ensuring that the disqualified or ineligible juror does not sit. In this respect an upsurge of concern over alleged jury nobbling has focused attention on those jurors who sit knowingly or unknowingly whilst disqualified and who may therefore be particularly vulnerable to the nobblers. Indeed, recent Home Office research[15] indicates that one in every 24 juries may contain a disqualified juror. In July 1988 it was announced that more spot checks would be undertaken to eradicate this problem.

The danger of police officers carrying out enquiries is that it opens the scope for other more sinister forms of vetting which cannot be monitored and for which there are no sanctions. We would therefore suggest that Criminal Records' Office checks are put in the hands of the Crown Court officers responsible for summoning the jury as part of their official duties. This would have the additional advantage of introducing an independent element into the checking process, a result which would be particularly desirable given the adversarial nature of the trial system. (In passing it should be noted that a former Lord Chancellor has announced that the Crown Courts are soon to be linked to the police national computer. It follows that the checking process we have described should be neither time-consuming nor expensive. It will also be accountable.)

What of other forms of vetting? Jury vetting by prosecutors takes place in America and many Australian states. (In most American states, however, the prosecution does not enjoy the luxury of majority verdicts.) In America defendants can counter the influence of vetting by taking an active part in the jury *voir dire* with a view to challenging for cause or without declaring reason. In Australia jury vetting suffers from many of the criticisms levelled at the Attorney-General's Guidelines, notably, the potential to create an imbalance between the prosecution and defence; lack of accountability; the invasion of juror privacy; and a heavy dependence on the good faith of the police.[16]

Arguably, vetting in England and Wales to establish extreme political bias is unnecessary not just because such jurors would be few and far between, but because the views of any juror would be absorbed within the jury and, if not, the majority verdict system would provide a further safeguard. In any event the vetting process for this purpose merely argues the case for the use of a jury *voir dire* in conjunction with the challenge for cause.

Security cases where evidence is likely to be given in camera represent the only arguable ground on which vetting can be based. It is said that jurors may, either voluntarily or under pressure, make improper use of evidence, although the number of these cases would seem to be few: the last such case was the Bettaney trial five years ago. (In the context of the Bettaney trial, it is difficult to see to what improper use such evidence could be put; after all, Bettaney had already passed the relevant material to the Russian Embassy.) If there is an argument for vetting on this count it has yet to be made out; regrettably the phrase 'the interests of national security' is all too often trotted out as a substitute for real argument.

Proposals for legislation

(1) Provision for Crown Court staff to have access to the police national computer in order to weed out disqualified jurors.
(2) Occupations of jurors to be included on the jury panel lists.
(3) Provision for a jury *voir dire* to eliminate active bias to be used in conjunction with the challenge for cause and the peremptory challenge (if it is ever restored).
(4) Creation of a criminal offence prohibiting any form of vetting not encompassed in the proposals above.

Chapter 4

Challenge

Trial by one's peers, even in its infancy, incorporated the right to challenge. In Cicero's Rome for instance, the law required accusor and accused to select 100 triers each. Each party would challenge 50 of his opponent's triers and the remaining 100 would try the case.[1]

When trial by jury developed in England the challenge emerged as a means of dealing with inherent bias in jurors and the danger of jury packing, which was rife until well into the last century. Several types of challenge developed to deal with these problems:

1 The challenge for cause; to the array (the panel of jurors) on the grounds of bias on the part of the Sheriff or some other irregularity in the empanelment; or to the polls (that is, to the individual jurors on the ground of some apparent or actual bias of a juror);
2 The prosecution right to stand-by jurors;
3 The peremptory challenge.

The challenge for cause

Challenge to the array – either party to a trial may challenge the array of jurors by showing cause

The onus of proof lies on the party who makes the challenge and the issue is determined by the trial judge. An important limitation on the challenge to the array is that one cannot cross-examine jurors without first establishing prima-facie evidence of bias by other means. A subsidiary rule is that jurors cannot be cross-examined on any matter 'tending to their dishonour'.

The challenge to the array has fallen into disuse. There has not been a successful challenge to the array in this century. The old cases tended to arise in three types of situation: first, where the Sheriff who summonsed the jury was the accusor or person aggrieved; secondly, where the jury had been selected on political or religious grounds; and thirdly where there was some semi-concealed relationship between one of the parties and the Sheriff (for instance, where the Sheriff was a member of a society funding the prosecution).[2] Responsibility for summoning of jurors now rests with the Lord Chancellor. Jurors are selected by the application of random numbers to the electoral role. It would seem that the old cases are unlikely to find modern parallels.

Bias, or the appearance of bias, is now likely to arise only by accident or in relation to race, which has taken the place of religion as a source of tension in society. Commonwealth jurisdictions produced, if not always for the best of reasons, solutions to trials involving racial or cultural issues. This was particularly relevant in those Commonwealth jurisdictions where tensions between settlers and native populations were always likely to arise. For instance, in Nigerian cases with non-native defendants up to one-half non-native jurors could be appointed. In the Gold Coast (where the jury numbered seven) in cases where there were non-native defendants a bare majority of non-native jurors could be appointed. In Johore a European defendant could require a majority of European jurors.[3] Equally, it should be noted that even in late Victorian England, a foreigner could obtain a jury '*de medietate linguae*', that is, a jury composed of an equal number of English and foreign jurors. This measure was introduced as long ago as 1353 and it remained on the statute book until 1870 when it was abolished on the ground that no alien need fear for a fair trial in England (perhaps an overly optimistic view, then as now). It is worth pointing out in this context that the appearance of a fair trial is almost as important as the fairness itself.[4]

In recent years, and until the intervention of the Court of Appeal in the summer of 1989, it seemed as though the English courts were beginning to readdress themselves to the problems of jury trial in a multi-racial society, where the defendant's culture or ethnic origins might have a specific bearing on the issues. It is worth looking at the line of authorities that developed.

At first it was a case of too little, too late. In *R. v. Broderick* (1970)[5] the Court of Appeal held that: 'a judge who directs that the panel shall include a coloured man to try a defendant who has indicated a desire for an all-coloured jury has gone as far as the law and consideration requires.'

Of more significance was the case of *Binns and others*.[6] Here twelve defendants were tried on charges of riotous assembly arising out of the St Paul's riots in Bristol in 1981. St Paul's was, and is, an area with a high proportion of people of ethnic minority background, particularly of West Indian origin. Relations between the police and many residents of the area had been poor for many years. Stocker J. accepted the proposition that 'the jury should contain a reasonable number of black people.' The judge held that: 'Nothwithstanding the wording of the Juries Act 1974, Section 11 (which refers to the selection of each jury by ballot in open court) ... where it appeared that the use of the peremptory challenge would not achieve a racially balanced jury, the trial judge may stand by jurors or allow the Crown to do so (if it is in agreement).' It seems clear that the trial judge was basing his decision on a development of earlier judicial authorities, but the underlying principle of this decision seems to be the duty of the judge to ensure a fair trial.

This bold approach was not followed in a number of subsequent cases but there were as many decisions for and against. In *Bansal*[7], a trial involving racial issues, Woolf J. achieved a multi-racial jury by a different approach. In this case he ordered the jury panel to be drawn from the Gravesend area of Kent which has a large Asian community. In *Fraser*[8], by some statistical fluke, the jury panel contained no coloured members though both the trial judge and the prosecution accepted that the issues raised in the case made it desirable to empanel a racially mixed jury. The result was achieved by the simple expedient of adjourning the trial for seven days.

This rather encouraging trend was recently halted by the Court of Appeal in the summer of 1989 when in the case of *Royston Ford*[9] it held that there was no statutory power or precedent at Common Law to authorise the empanelment of a multiracial jury. Certainly, the Court of Appeal was correct in holding there was no statutory basis for such a discretion because the summoning of jurors is the responsibility of the Lord Chancellor.[10] The Court did consider some of the older authorities, notably *R. v. Mansell*[11] in which it was held that a judge could discharge a juror to prevent 'scandal or perversion' including, perhaps, a juror who was unwell or deaf. However, continued the Court of Appeal, the rule in *Mansell* 'had never been held to include a discretion to discharge a jury drawn from particular sections of the community, or otherwise to influence the overall composition of the jury'.

It is possible the Court of Appeal may have erred on this point. The principle in *Mansell* was not derived from any arcane law relating to the excusal of jurors but rather from the inherent duty of a trial judge to ensure a fair trial. Our judges have not been shy of extending the scope of the common law when it suits them. It could have been extended to meet the justice of this situation.

Challenge to the polls – either party to a trial may mount unlimited challenges for cause to individual jurors

The rules as to procedure and determination of the challenge to the polls are broadly the same as those governing the challenge to the array. In particular, the rule that jurors cannot be questioned to establish cause, unless the defendant can by other means adduce prima-facie evidence to support a challenge for cause, is rigidly applied. Clearly, that is extremely difficult to do. It seems that the last occasion when leave to cross-examine jurors for cause was successfully sought occurred in the second trial of Ronald Kray. It was successfully argued on behalf of Kray that the publicity arising out of the first trial was so widespread and of such an adverse character that it amounted to prima-facie evidence of bias in the jury panel.[12] Lawton J. reluctantly agreed. Lawton later wrote:

> I had experience of this in the second part of the Kray trial. At the end of the first part the press reported the result and two newspapers gave accounts of how some of the defendants were alleged to have behaved, which had never been the subject matter of any charges. The consequence was that when I started the second part, counsel for the defendants referred to by the newspapers in this way queried whether they could get a fair trial. After considering some ancient authorities ... I allowed a very limited amount of cross-examination of the jurors as they came to be sworn. But I found the whole procedure very unsatisfactory.[13]

It is significant that this is the last case on the point and is now some 20 years old. The effect of the strict implementation of the rules relating to the cross-examination of jurors has rendered the challenge for cause almost obsolete. It is perhaps an example of precedent inhibiting the development of the law to meet new problems.

This is in stark contrast to the position in, for instance, America, where the philosophy of challenging is fundamentally different. Counsel is permitted to question jurors extensively on the *voir dire* in order to make out a challenge. In some cases this process has been known to take weeks or even months. At the recent trial of Oliver North it took a modest eight days to empanel a jury.

Jessica Mitford once described the purposes of the American *voir dire* as:

> a three-pronged thrust: (1) to eliminate via the challenge for cause those jurors who through their answers demonstrate to the judge's satisfaction that they are prejudiced against the politics or race of the defendant; (2) to spot out those jurors whom it would be wise to exclude via the peremptory challenge; and (3) to educate the whole panel who are sitting there in open court as to the issues in the case.[14]

The third of these grounds is anathema to the ears of English courts, the second only marginally less so, but it is more difficult to argue against the first proposition.

None the less, English courts have determinedly resisted any drift towards the American style *voir dire*, preferring instead to reiterate the principle of random selection. However, there have been a few occasions where English courts make exceptions within the scope of the Practice Direction where a juror is 'personally concerned in the facts of the particular case, or closely connected with a party to the proceedings'.

The Angry Brigade trial is one example. Eight young people were charged with conspiracy to cause explosions. It was said they were members of a far left terrorist organisation and that this was their motivation for planting a number of bombs in the homes of politicians, in embassies, and in banks.

At the instance of defence counsel, Mr Justice James put a number of questions to the jurors, including such matters as: Were any jurors subscribing members of the Conservative Party or members of the Territorial Army? Had any jurors formed the view that the defendants were members of the Angry Brigade? If so, could they put that impression out of their minds? It seems that the questions were put to the jury panel *en bloc*. They were not required to answer individually, merely to excuse themselves from service if they came within any of the excepted categories or felt they might be biased. Despite the rather unsatisfactory method adopted, as many as 19 jurors asked to be excused. (One imagines that a juror harbouring real bias would be unlikely to excuse himself.)

In any event, it was in response to this development that the Lord Chief Justice issued the Practice Direction the following year, emphasising that the principle of random selection was paramount. The principle of random selection continues to represent the state of the law, though there have still been circumstances when trial judges have been prepared to excuse jurors for possible bias. *R. v. Silcott and Others*[15] was one such trial. This concerned the murder of Police Constable Blakelock during the Broadwater Farm riot. Jurors who had close relatives or friends who were police officers were invited to excuse themselves, as were jurors who had family or friends living on the Broadwater estate. Ten jurors were excused.

The stand-by

The prosecution has the right to stand-by jurors until the panel of jurors is exhausted. If the panel becomes exhausted in this way and the jury is still not complete, the jurors who have been stood-by are called again. On being recalled, the prosecution must either accept the jurors or mount challenges for cause.

Since the panel often number 100 or more, the effect of the rule is to give the prosecution far greater potential than the defence to influence the composition of the jury. Although used commonly in the 1960s and 1970s, the stand-by is now rarely exercised, but since it tends to be employed in conjunction with jury vetting it can potentially be used to telling effect. We have already pointed out in Chapter 3 that the use of the stand-by has been severely curtailed by recent guidelines issued by the Attorney-General. The stand-by may now only be used in two instances. Firstly where a juror is manifestly unsuitable and the defence agrees to the use of the stand-by. Secondly, in security or terrorist cases as a consequence of a vetting authorised by the Attorney-General's Guidelines on jury vetting.[16]

The peremptory challenge

This has now been abolished in England and Wales by the Criminal Justice Act 1988, section 118. At the time of the abolition any defendant tried by a jury was entitled to three peremptory challenges. The prosecution has not enjoyed the use of the peremptory challenge in this jurisdiction since the fourteenth century. It has, of course, had the right of stand-by.

In cases where several defendants stood trial together a concerted use of the peremptory challenge by defence counsel could exercise considerable influence on the composition of the jury, although, of course, as each juror was challenged, the replacement juror was drawn at random from the remainder of the panel.

In the middle to late 1960s there was a resurgence in the use of the challenge after a period of many years when it remained moribund. It seems that the rare use of the challenge was attributable to the juror property qualification which meant that one potential juror was much like another. The few women who were summoned to do jury service were often challenged in cases where it was alleged by the police that the defendant had sworn during his interviews. The basis for the challenge, perhaps chauvinist, perhaps irrational, and certainly unsupported, was that they would be prejudiced against a man who constantly used four-letter words. It was possibly due also to the fact that counsel who understood run-of-the-mill criminal work were less inclined to combative defence tactics.

Professor Cornish records the first stirrings of concern arising over the case of *William and Others* in 1965. In this case the five defendants exercised a large number of peremptory challenges, acting directly and not, as was usual, through their counsel. During the course of the trial a number of jurors reported attempts made to bribe them into recording verdicts of acquittal. Cornish speculated that: 'Unscrupulous defendants are using their peremptory challenges . . . to remove jurors who look intelligent and who would therefore be less susceptible to bribes or intimidation.'

In the years that followed, the peremptory challenge came to be used more aggressively, as indeed did the prosecution stand-by. This was particularly so after the abolition of the property qualification.

The questioning of jurors in the Angry Brigade trial coupled with the aggressive use of the peremptory challenge led to the Lord Chief Justice's Practice Direction which reiterated that the principle of random selection was paramount. The same year the Lord Chancellor directed that the occupation of jurors should no longer appear on jury panel lists. The rationale for this was that challenging jurors on the sole basis of their occupation was an abuse. Challenging of accountants in fraud cases was cited as an example.

This view can be balanced by the counter-argument succinctly put by Lord Justice Lawton: 'I regret that defence counsel no longer know the occupations of jurors. In my time at the Bar the right to challenge was rarely exercised and when it was it was usually to remove from the jury someone who was likely to have specialised knowledge relating to the charge. I thought they would have too great an influence in the juryroom.'[17]

The debate over the use of the peremptory challenge was sustained by trenchant criticism, notably by Judge Alan King Hamilton and Sir Robert Mark, who later wrote of one notable trial of the period that 'the right of peremptory challenge exercised by skilful counsel had ensured a jury virtually certain to acquit.'[18] And at Westminster, Lord Mansfield described his own experience as a defence lawyer when he used the peremptory challenge to get 'a layabout lot of unemployed males'.[19] It is now clear that wearing a suit or carrying a copy of *The Times* or *Telegraph* was often sufficient to warrant a challenge.

Opinion at the Bar as to the efficacy of the challenge was divided. Many barristers saw themselves as fine exponents of the art of the challenge. Others were less sure and thought it an unpredictable tool and even counter-productive, making jurors suspicious and determined to prove their independence.

Arguments for the peremptory challenge

(1) It is a useful tool where, for instance, a defendant suspects bias in a juror which he is unable to prove. The exercise of the peremptory challenge in such circumstances helps to ensure that the defendant feels he has had a fair trial. This is an important consideration even, or especially, where the suspicion is unreasonable. The case of Tyndale is one good example.

John Tyndale, former Chairman of the British National Party, and John Morse, were indicted on charges of conspiracy to cause racial hatred by publishing a number of issues of a magazine, the *British Nationalist*. A number of articles in the magazine contained attacks on ethnic minorities. Three jurors were challenged, one of whom was black, another Asian and the third, apparently Jewish. In this case the challenges were to no avail, because the all-white jury convicted Tyndale and his co-defendant, although it is argued that the use of the challenge denied Mr Tyndale the opportunity of suggesting that he was unfairly treated.

(2) It is desirable that defendants are not tried by juries which, through some hiccup in the summoning process, suffer from an age, sex, or racial imbalance. On this point it is well to remember that our society is no longer homogeneous, and a number of ethnic minorities flourish in our cities which often maintain distinctive cultural ties and outlook. There ought, therefore, to be a provision capable

of remedying any such imbalance in a jury. We note in passing Baldwin and McConville's observation in their study of juries in Birmingham, which indicated that women, West Indian, Pakistani, and Irish were significantly under-represented on juries in proportion to their numbers in the local population. Baldwin and McConville were unable to identify any reason for such imbalances save for 'informal selection procedures ... by junior administrative staff'.[20]

(3) Where a defendant faces a series of trials, the peremptory challenge is a simple expedient for avoiding 'jury contamination'; for example, where one or more jurors have tried a defendant once and find themselves inadvertently recalled to try the same defendant on a subsequent trial. The peremptory challenge covers the problem without alerting other jurors to the defendant's 'past'. For the same reasons, challenge for cause is cumbersome and inappropriate.

(4) It allows redress against deliberate interference with the random summoning of jurors. David Cocks QC, writing in *Counsel*, related that: 'It is certainly within the recent memory of many members of the Bar that juries at one particular London Court would be summarily dismissed if they acquitted ... whilst convicting juries would be kept together throughout the session.'[21]

Two other arguments were advanced. First, if a defendant had a right to challenge without giving reasons, then the exercise of that right ought not to be questioned. Second, if any abuse was taking place, then the sensible course of action would be to identify and curb abuse rather than abolish the challenge completely.

Regrettably the arguments against abolition were not widely appreciated and received little attention from the media, although allegations of abuse of the challenge continued to receive sensationalist coverage. Matters finally came to a head after the trial of seven RAF servicemen in what became known as the Cyprus Spy case. In 1985 these seven young men were tried at the Old Bailey on charges alleging that they had passed state secrets to the Eastern Bloc. It was said that they had been enticed into homosexual orgies and afterwards blackmailed into revealing military secrets to Eastern Bloc agents. Twelve jurors were challenged by defence counsel acting in concert. All the defendants were acquitted by the jury.

Certain sections of the press and various backbench MP's took this as proof positive that the peremptory challenge was being used to pack juries in favour of acquittals. In fact the point may have been an unfair one in the context of the Cyprus Spy Trial, not least because the entire panel of jurors had been vetted on behalf of the prosecution by a branch of M.I.5. Also, on any view the prosecution case was weak, consisting solely of confessions which each defendant maintained had been obtained by duress. A government enquiry later condemned the interrogation techniques used.

The 'packing' theory also ignores the fact that it is largely in the hands of the prosecution as to how many defendants are tried on the same indictment. There are financial, tactical and evidential advantages to the prosecution in trying a number of defendants together. If in these circumstances defendants pooled challenges, this may have been a legitimate tactic.

In any event, Hansard records that on November 7, 1985 the following exchange took place between Toby Jessel MP and the Home Secretary:

Jessel: Do not the police believe that they are handicapped in their efforts to prevent and deter crime because the abuse of the right to challenge the membership of juries means they are distorted in favour of too many acquittals . . . ?

Mr Hurd: . . . I have been in contact with law officers who found they do not have sufficient information for action . . . The Attorney-General will be arranging for the new Crown Prosecution Service . . . to conduct such a survey so that we have a basis of fact upon which we can consider whether action is needed.

Astonishingly and regrettably, before the results of the survey by the Crown Prosecution Service were known, the Home Secretary introduced the Criminal Justice Bill of 1986 setting out the Government's intention to abolish the peremptory challenge. The Home Secretary soon found himself with egg on his face. The results of the exhaustive Crown Prosecution Service survey disclosed no link between the use of the challenge and acquittal rates. The survey also found that the practice of pooling challenges in multi-handed cases was, at most, rare. The Government pressed on with the abolition of the peremptory challenge. Was the abolition justified or was it merely a symbolic crusade? Certainly, if the challenge was being used to load juries with individuals unable or unwilling to carry out their duties, since this would be an abuse of the system. But the evidence in support of this theory was, at best, slight and anecdotal.

There were a number of reasons why the peremptory challenge ought to have been retained. First, the various functions of the peremptory challenge as already described were never disputed by the Government. Second, no alternative mechanism has been introduced to deal with, for instance, age, sex, or racial imbalance in a jury. Third, the abolition of the peremptory challenge must be viewed in the context of an adversarial system of justice, in which the prosecution right of stand-by remains intact. Fourth, the decision to abolish flew in the face of all the expert evidence received by the Government; in particular, the views of the Law Society, the Criminal Bar Association and the Crown Prosecution Service survey.[22] Fifth, the decision to abolish the peremptory challenge is at odds with the practice of other countries which retain jury trial. For instance in America, Australia and France the peremptory challenge continues to be an integral part of the trial system. Finally, the rationale of the abolition is questionable. The White Paper of 1986 on Criminal Justice stated that the peremptory challenge was being 'used as a means of getting rid of jurors whose mere appearance is thought to indicate a degree of insight or respect for the law which is inimical to the interests of the defence'.

In fact, most challenging took place because defendants in the criminal process tend to be both young and from disadvantaged backgrounds. It is not surprising, therefore, that many defence lawyers challenged in an attempt to produce a jury which was in touch with the life-style, the problems, and the culture of defendants.

Of course, there was also that section of the Bar which challenged, in the spirit described by Lord Mansfield: 'to get a layabout lot of unemployed males'; a line of reasoning which presupposes a dearth of honest decent people of integrity and reasonable intelligence. It also presupposes that the absence of these qualities is readily apparent from a short visual inspection. It appears to have been the logic of the Government's point of view that a sufficiently vigorous use of the challenge will eventually throw up a jury unwilling, or unfitted, to do justice between State and defendant.

It is debatable whether the age, sex, class, religion, or racial background of jurors affects the verdicts juries return. We need to attempt to answer this question at this stage. In attempting to answer this question the relationship between the social composition of juries and the verdicts they return can be discussed in relation to the following points:

(1) The abolition of the juror property qualification in this country;
(2) The influence of the peremptory challenge on verdicts;
(3) The American experience of the *voir dire* and the challenge.

(1) *The abolition of the juror property qualification.* As already mentioned, this was abolished in 1972 on the recommendations of the Morris Committee. Hitherto the jury tended to be middle-class, middle-aged, male, and white. In the aftermath of abolition the social composition of juries changed dramatically in terms of age, sex, class, and race.

What effect did this have on verdicts? A Home Office study carried out immediately after the implementation of the legislation compared acquittal rates for a three-month period before and after the reform and found no significant change in acquittal rates.[23] A more recent Home Office study of acquittal rates confirms the experience of practitioners that the rate varies from circuit to circuit and within circuit. (Incidentally, most criminal practitioners regard Snaresbrook Crown Court to be particularly good for acquittals.) The Home Office study (*Acquittal Rates*)[24] noted that the acquittal rates had crept up. The report suggested a number of explanations and concluded that 'there is little evidence to show whether or not broadening of eligibility for jury service ... has led to an increased propensity for the jury to acquit'. Significantly, Baldwin and McConville's study did not establish any link between the characteristics of juries in terms of age, sex, and class and the verdicts being returned.

Sealy and Cornish have carried out other research[25] with mock juries in an attempt to establish links between the attributes of jurors, in terms of age, sex, occupation, educational achievement, and previous experience of the law. Their conclusions were that over the broad spectrum of offences there was no link between social composition of jurors and verdicts save that younger jurors tended to acquit more readily.

(2) *The influence of the peremptory challenge on acquittal rates.* The academic research to which we have alluded would seem to suggest that a vigorous use of the peremptory challenge would lead to young juries which would be more likely to acquit and, whilst any mock jury research must be treated with caution, the research of Sealy and Cornish is corroborated by the practical experience of a substantial number of practising criminal lawyers.

On the other hand, the recent Crown Prosecution Service survey on the use of the peremptory challenge, which involved a study of 3,165 cases over a 15-month period, indicated no correlation between acquittal rates and the use of the peremptory challenge.

(3) *The American experience of the* voir dire *and the challenge.* In

the Angela Davis case three psychologists were employed by the defence to assist in screening jurors before the *voir dire* process began. Dozens of volunteers were enlisted to conduct a detailed investigation of the panel of jurors by checking their political affiliations, social backgrounds, and jobs on a scale unmatched in this country (save perhaps by the security services in Official Secrets trials). Jessica Mitford noted that one over-enthusiastic volunteer even went so far as to chart the astrological signs of each member of the jury panel: 'Virgo rising in the fourth quarter, etc.'

The trial arising out of the siege of Wounded Knee and the trial of the Harrisburg Six provide classic examples of cases in which defence teams carried out in-depth studies of the kind of jurors who would be favourable or unfavourable to their cause.[26] The Harrisburg six included a number of priests and nuns and a Pakistani. They were accused of plotting to cause explosions, raid draft boards, and kidnap Henry Kissinger as part of an anti-Vietnam war campaign.

The trial was preceded by a painstaking sociological study of the jury catchment area. The jury *voir dire* lasted three weeks. The defence got it wrong in respect of two jurors at least. One, Lawrence Evans, had said of the defendants during the *voir dire* 'I couldn't be against hippies because I have sons who look like that.' Kathryn Swartz, a mother of four and a conscientious objector, was persuaded by Evans to vote for a conviction. The jury 'hung' and a mistrial was declared. (This is not an isolated case. During the trial of Colonel Oliver North it came to light that three jurors had lied during the *voir dire* in order to ensure they were not challenged off.)[27]

It is interesting to note the reactions of the great American trial lawyers (Belli, Darrow, and others) to potential jurors and who makes a good man, or sometimes woman, in the jury-box. In *Inside the Jury*[28] the authors encapsulate the words of wisdom garnered over the years by the cream of the American defence Bar. Here are the thoughts and advice of those great advocates: '... attorneys are told to avoid jurors having a special knowledge of areas about which expert witnesses will testify, for these jurors will think they know more than the other jurors and the experts' (Heyl). This view was shared by Lord Justice Lawton who bemoaned the 1973 decision that the jurors' occupations be removed from the jury list. E.L.Biskind disagreed: 'The defence should accept jurors with the same occupation as the defendant.' B.E.Davis and R.E.Wiley agreed with Heyl and Lawton.

There follows some of the most fascinating contradictory

information ever garnered from textbooks for lawyers. Just who on a jury is likely to be sympathetic towards the defence? It is really a question of paying your money and taking your choice. J. White, jun. thought 'the unemployed, pensioners, and people on relief are thought to be generous but teachers, clergy, and lawyers should generally be rejected'. And: 'Farmers are desirable for criminal prosecution and civil defense, for they believe in strict liability, whereas waiters and bartenders are forgiving.' Not too surprisingly, bankers were regarded as bad for criminal defendants in robbery and theft cases but, perhaps more controversially, were thought to be good in white-collar crime trials. F. L. Bailey and H. B. Rothblatt were quite firm on the subject. Unless the defendant is a veteran with a good military record, retired police, military men, and their wives are undesirable, for they adhere to strict codes.

But what about objecting to the men or women on the jury? In England it has been the practice to try for an all-male jury in sex cases, as was the case in the days when drink-driving cases could be tried by a jury. But American trial lawyers have very definite and conflicting views. Clarence Darrow should know: 'avoid women in all defence cases'. His view on this matter, however, was not shared by other American trial lawyers.

In the case of race and nationality American lawyers were not so divided; never drop an Irish person for the Irish identify with defendants. Nordic, English, Scandinavian, and German jurors are preferred if it is necessary to combat emotional appeals. With regard to social and marital status, Belli thought married people best for criminal defendants on the basis they were more experienced in life and more forgiving. On age, younger people were said to favour the defendant. Certainly, this is the view of many English trial lawyers, borne out by the research of Sealey and Cornish. Again, this was a view shared by Adkins. As to wealth, Darrow's view was that the wealthy were prone to convict save in white-collar criminal cases. And the vexed subject of religion? Darrow had strong views: Presbyterians are too cold and should be avoided in defence cases; Baptists are even less desirable. Jews, Unitarians, Universalists, Congregationalists, and agnostics should be retained. However, if that appears to be definitive, Appleman thinks otherwise. His view is that information on religion is not normally helpful.

The American experience would seem to indicate that the jury *voir dire* is a useful tool for sifting out jurors who may be positively biased. We are not convinced that it has any of the greater uses attributed to it by many American trial lawyers. In particular, there is no evidence that the jury *voir dire* appreciably affects acquittal rates. It does undoubtedly avoid injustice or the appearance of injustice in individual cases.

The evidence relating to this jurisdiction suggests (in general) that the social composition of juries does not affect verdicts save that there is agreement that younger juries are more likely to acquit. Again, the real value of the peremptory challenge would appear to lie in avoiding injustice or the appearance of injustice in individual cases.

The future of the challenge

The present position is somewhat bleak. The peremptory challenge has been abolished; the challenge for cause is all but obsolete. Only the prosecution, through the stand-by, has the means of influencing the composition of the jury.

It is naive to equate random selection with lack of bias or to hope blindly that one juror's prejudice will be cancelled out by the good sense of another. Under the present system the only safeguard one has is the good will of individual trial judges who, very occasionally, can be persuaded to ask one or two questions of the jury panel with a view to excusing those jurors who may have some close connection with one of the parties.

In our view there are two problems which need to be dealt with. Firstly, eliminating actual bias. Secondly, eliminating apparent bias. For instance, to take a crude example, if a defendant were charged with assault on a police officer it would be unfortunate if any of the jurors trying the case were related to, or friends of, a police officer.

Examples of potential bias abound. We have already noted the danger of racial bias, be it deliberate or through ignorance. The recent decision of the Court of Appeal outlawing the practice of empanelling multiracial juries is to be regretted. The decision was based in part on the refusal of the Court of Appeal to extend the scope of the rule in the case of Mansell which was decided in 1857. (In passing it ought to be noted that a coloured defendant tried at the time of Mansell would have been able to obtain a jury *de medietate linguae*. Such a defendant could also have influenced the composition of the jury through the use of the peremptory challenge. Neither of these options are now available to defendants.)

Another example of potential bias arose out of the 1984 miners' strike. There was much bitterness between the striking miners and the strike breakers. Pennington, a striking miner, was tried and convicted of an offence committed on the picket line.[29] After his conviction he appealed on the ground that it had come to light that one of the jurors was a working miner. His appeal was dismissed but the Court of Appeal approved a direction given in a similar case. In that case Judge Jolly had asked any juror on the panel to withdraw if they had an interest in the strike. It is perhaps an example of the Court of Appeal recognising the possibility of bias but refusing to take any steps to obviate it.

There is a strong argument for the reintroduction of the peremptory challenge and a relaxation of the rules governing the challenge for cause. Both of these should be used in conjunction with a limited *voir dire*. We do not propose the introduction of the *voir dire* on the scale it is used in America, which is clearly expensive, overly time-consuming, and after a certain point speculative and even futile. The scope of questions to be asked on the *voir dire* could be thrashed out between judge and counsel before the trial. The empanelment of the jury need not take significantly longer.

Chapter 5

Majority Verdicts

It may be that the most momentous reform of the jury system in recent years was occasioned by the Criminal Justice Act of 1967 which abolished the unanimity rule.[1] The reform, re-enacted by Section 17 of the Juries Act 1974, empowers a trial judge to accept a majority verdict after a jury has been deliberating for at least two hours or 'such longer period as the court thinks reasonable having regard to the nature and complexity of the case'. In practice the jury is always allowed at least two hours and ten minutes before a majority direction is given.

Section 17 of the 1974 Act stipulates that the permitted majorities are: (a) in a case where there are not less than eleven jurors, ten of whom agree on the verdict, and (b) in a case where there are ten jurors, nine of whom agree on the verdict. The reference to eleven and ten jurors is calculated to take account of the possibility of one or two jurors being discharged during the trial through incapacity or misconduct.

The unanimity rule

The rule requiring unanimity can be traced back some 600 years.[2] Lord Devlin once explained the rationale of the rule in these eloquent terms: 'The criminal verdict is based on the absence of reasonable doubt. If there were a dissenting minority of a third or a quarter, that would of itself suggest to the popular mind the existence of a reasonable doubt'.[3] Stephen J. had this to say: 'My own opinion is that trial by jury has both merits and defects but that the unanimity required by the jurors is essential to it. If that is to be given up, the institution itself should be abolished.'[4] These views once represented what one might term the mainstream opinion on the requirement for unanimity. They reflect the origins of the rule when jurors gave their verdict by swearing an oath in favour of one or other parties.

The retention of the rule owed much to the laudable stance that punishment (perhaps death or imprisonment) must be the consequence of proof which was clear enough to satisfy beyond reasonable doubt twelve randomly selected individuals. Clearly, the unanimity rule was fundamental to the system. Its endurance for 600 years makes the introduction of majority verdicts one of the most significant reforms of the jury system in centuries.

Majority verdicts: the debate

Why then was this reform necessary? Lord Denning explains: 'The reasoning for the change was impressive. It was based on the new type of crime. This was highly organised by men who robbed banks and stole huge sums of money. If they were charged one of their friends or associates would try to bribe or threaten one of the jurors or his wife or relatives ... Time after time this happened.'[5]

This has come to represent the orthodox view of the necessity for introducing majority verdicts. It is in fact the stuff of which myths are made. 'Nobbling' was not 'a new type of crime'; the Common Law offence of embracery is as old as the jury system itself and crops up regularly in the history of the jury. There is no evidence that in the mid-1960s attempts to nobble jurors were made 'time after time'. The evidence presented to Parliament indicated that a few isolated attempts had been made. No evidence was presented to show that any such attempt had been successful. The then Home Secretary, Roy Jenkins, stated that 'the Commissioner of Police informed me at the beginning of August that he knew, without close investigation ... of six major cases in the Metropolitan Police District over the past three years'.[6]

Six cases in three years is hardly evidence upon which to abolish a fundamental rule of law. And did the Commissioner of Police stir himself (since the previous August) to investigate the scale of the problem? It seems not. Were the six cases referred to really attempts to nobble the jury and were they successful? No evidence other than a passing reference to one trial was forthcoming.

Another argument advanced was the expense and inconvenience of hung juries. The force of this argument has become apparent in the last 30 years as trials have become progressively longer. It was once very unusual for a trial to last more than a month; it is now commonplace. In such a trial the expense to the public purse is huge, and if the jury hangs this in itself is a factor which may persuade the prosecution not to proceed to a retrial. It was argued that no single individual ought to possess this power. This was a view that had been gaining ground for many years, and of course there is a wealth of anecdotal evidence relating to stubborn or unreasonable jurors. Interestingly, however, there is almost no evidence of corrupt jurors.

The difficulties of getting twelve jurors to agree has long been a problem for the judiciary. The old rule that jurors should have no refreshment during their deliberations (which we have described in Chapter I) was an effective if crude measure to this end.[7] When this rule died a natural, if protracted, death, other means of coaxing unanimous verdicts had to be found. When a jury was in danger of 'hanging' many members of the judiciary sought to find a form of words which might help to break the deadlock. To this end the 'Walhein direction' was given for many years.[8] It was usually couched in these terms: 'There must necessarily be argument and a certain amount of give and take and adjustment of views within the scope of the oath you have taken; and it makes for great inconvenience and expense if jurors cannot agree owing to the unwillingness of one of their number to listen to the arguments of the rest. Having said that ... if you disagree in your verdict you must say so.' The Walhein direction was originally concerned with the single dissenting juror who might hold out and cause a retrial. In any event, there had been a growing body of opinion that 'the man whose spiritual home is in the minority of one' should not be allowed to prevail.[9]

Roy Jenkins professed not to hold this view but noted that hung juries occurred in nearly 4% of criminal trials in England and Wales in 1965.[10] Jenkins asserted that many of these hung because 'one or two had been persuaded by bribery or intimidation to hold out against the evidence'. This suggestion is puzzling, for no evidence was produced to show that any jury had hung for that reason. As far as we can discover there was not a single conviction or even a prosecution of any individual for juror interference during this period.

More pressing reasons for the introduction of majority verdicts included the expense and inconvenience of retrials, and an unstated desire to bolster the conviction rate. We have already dealt with the public purse argument. It is only necessary to add that there was a strong body of opinion at the time that too many criminals were avoiding conviction. This was certainly a viewpoint held by the Metropolitan Police Commissioner, Robert Mark, who was particularly outspoken on the subject. Robert Mark and the Association of Chief Police Officers were instrumental in collating and publishing the results of a survey which purported to show jury acquittals were running at an unacceptably high figure of 39%. As always, timing is all-important in these matters; the results were published in the *New Law Journal* in June 1966, only a few months before the Criminal Justice Bill was laid before Parliament.

Some years later the results of the police survey were to be completely discredited; but the damage had already been done. The survey caused considerable disquiet and paved the way for Home Secretary Roy Jenkins to introduce legislation on the seemingly altruistic ground of preventing interference with juries. Findley and Duff suggest that factors relating to conviction rates and cost to the public purse may have weighed far more heavily than the Government of the day cared to admit.[11]

A further argument which had a superficial attraction was that other jurisdictions employing jury systems also allowed majority verdicts. Notable examples include Scotland, France, and certain American and Australian states. There are, however, difficulties in making such comparisons; for instance, the Scottish system allows a verdict by a bare majority which makes it almost impossible to successfully interfere with a jury. Scottish juries may return three verdicts; guilty, not guilty and not proven; the problems of hung juries therefore do not arise. It is also noteworthy that Scotland has a larger jury and different rules of evidence.

Comparisons with non-British jurisdictions were based on a false premise: that these other countries have or had in common with England the same understanding of the purpose of a criminal trial. Many have said that the purpose of the criminal trial in England is to acquit the innocent. It has been said that it is better that ten guilty men be acquitted than one innocent man be convicted. These are noble sentiments, but very few foreign jurisdictions share this order of priorities. Even so, arguments based on comparisons with other countries carried some weight in the debate.

In any event, these secondary arguments would hardly have pre-
vailed but for a combination of two other factors. First, the abolition
of the death penalty the previous year somehow made the reform
more palatable. It is certainly the case that in jurisdictions which
allowed capital punishment, unanimity was still strongly preferred.
In Scotland, for example, Alec Brown records that 'from 1900–48
47% of those convicted of murder in Scotland by unanimous verdict
were executed, but only 33% of those convicted by majority'. A second
factor was the isolated number of juror intimidation, which gave a
spurious legitimacy to the campaign for majority verdicts.

Alternatives to majority verdicts

If jury nobbling was a problem or at least perceived to be a problem
in the 1960s, what were the various solutions? Undoubtedly, the introduction of majority verdicts was one solution but it clearly ought
to have been a measure of the last resort. Some other measures were
adopted: protection was given to jurors thought to be vulnerable;
and a hotline was set up for jurors who might be threatened. These
were temporary measures, however, and did not deal with the causes
of the problem.

One other reform was introduced by the Criminal Justice Act of
1967 – the disqualification from jury service of persons who had served
a sentence of imprisonment. Such individuals were (rightly) thought
to be vulnerable to corruption. This reform might well have been
sufficient in itself to deal with the nobbling problem. One might
argue that it ought to have been tried and its efficacy assessed before
resorting to the introduction of majority verdicts.

Another argument came to light some years after majority verdicts
were made law. It is clear now that jury vetting was being carried
out on a fairly widespread basis during the 1960s. If one is to believe
the arguments in favour of jury vetting as a means of weeding out
biased or potentially corrupt jurors then this ought to have been sufficient protection in itself. This argument remains relevant. It is a
matter of regret that the secrecy surrounding vetting contributed to
the view that there was no viable alternative but to introduce majority
verdicts.

There were other steps which could have been introduced to deal
with the nobblers (if indeed they represented a serious threat). Such
measures could have included ensuring that jurors remained

anonymous prior to trial, out of sight of the public gallery during the trial, and the reintroduction in certain exceptional circumstances of sequestrating jurors. We discuss juror protection in more detail in Chapter 8 in the context of jury trial in Northern Ireland and in Chapter 10 in more general terms. At this stage it is only necessary to point out that no consideration was given to the alternatives to majority verdicts.

It might be said that the complete absence of any discussion of proposals short of abolishing the unanimity rule was the most significant feature of the debate. If the integrity of the jury system had been the real issue, other ways of dealing with this problem would have been found or at least canvassed. One can only assume (with Messrs Findley and Duff) that the Government's real concern focussed on increasing conviction rates and saving on the cost of retrials.

Consequences of introducing majority verdicts

The reform was introduced ostensibly to deal with the problems of hung juries and jury nobbling. We have argued that a more pressing concern was to increase the conviction rate. Did the reform achieve its aims?

Perhaps the most striking result of the reform was that convictions became easier to obtain. During the first six months of the operation of majority verdicts, 1 October 1967 to 31 March 1968, 223 people were convicted on majority verdicts by juries. This figure represented 1.8% of all those convicted by juries.[12] Twenty-three years later majority convictions are so commonplace as to be unremarkable.

The situation was exacerbated by the Walhein direction which continued to be given until it was finally disapproved by the Court of Appeal in 1988.[13] The direction may now be given only if it contains no reference to 'the expense and inconvenience' of hung juries.

The introduction of majority verdicts may have resulted in many more convictions but it did not resolve the problem of hung juries. Although there are no statistics on the incidence of hung juries anecdotal evidence suggests that the introduction of majority verdicts has made no appreciable inroad into the number of hung juries.

Nor did the reform succeed entirely in alleviating concern over jury nobbling, though it did make the possibility much more remote – the nobblers now have to corrupt or intimidate three jurors to be sure of success. However, according to the Metropolitan Police this has not deterred the nobblers; they have simply become more proficient and ruthless in recent years. This phenomenon is discussed in more detail in Chapter 10.

Conclusions

It is difficult to avoid the conclusion that the decision to introduce majority verdicts had more to do with considerations of cost, efficiency, and a more acceptable conviction rate than with preserving the integrity of the jury system. As we have said, there were alternative methods of combating the jury nobblers which, by and large, were never tried let alone canvassed.

Perhaps the strongest argument against the introduction of majority verdicts has been put forward by Professor Cornish: 'the real strength of the case against the majority system lies in the possibility of a jury in which only one or two members can see an obstacle to conviction.' Of course it does not follow that the one or two jurors holding out are unreasonable or even wrong. The force of this argument may not have been readily apparent when majority verdicts were introduced. As society becomes more culturally and racially diverse it becomes more likely that defendants may find themselves tried by a jury with whom they have little in common. The customs, circumstances, and experiences of life of one ethnic grouping may be anathema to other ethnic minorities living in the same neighbourhood. This, of course, is an argument for the peremptory challenge and it illustrates the origins of the jury *de medietate linguae* which is discussed in Chapter 4. The lesson of history would appear to be that the more culturally fragmented society becomes the greater the need for unanimity of verdict.

This last point may be of particular importance when one considers how juries are likely to approach their deliberations. Jurors are always told during the course of summing up that a majority verdict can be given at some later stage. Common sense dictates that despite a judicial direction to seek unanimity, once ten or eleven jurors are agreed real debate will grind to a halt.

The effect of the reform has been to undermine the standard of proof. Take for example a case in which a jury deliberates for some hours or even days before returning to convict by a majority of 10–2. It is not possible to split the two dissenting jurors and condemn them as illogical, wrong, or unreasonable. All one can say is that the jury as a whole is possessed of a doubt and the prosecution has failed to discharge the burden of proof.

It is unlikely that any future administration will be persuaded to undertake a return to unanimous verdicts. It has not been possible to point to any disintegration of public confidence in jury verdicts which flows directly from this reform. It also seems unlikely that any Government is going to have the gumption to face up to the fact that majority verdicts are fundamentally inconsistent with the concept of proof beyond reasonable doubt. Perhaps majority verdicts were the necessary price to pay for the abolition of the property qualification. As such this reform is probably the lesser of two evils.

Faced with this rather bleak scenario, we offer two halfway-house reforms. The first is that no person shall be convicted of a crime where more than one juror dissents. The second alternative reform is one suggested by Paul Byrne who observes that: 'The interrelationship between the requirements of unanimity and proof beyond reasonable doubt is clear. Based on this association, there is ... an entirely logical argument in favour of permitting acquittals by majority but not convictions ... the notion of acquittal by a majority does not offend any of the powerful arguments of principle which favour the preservation of unanimity.'[14]

In essence this means that where a jury hangs 8–4 or 9–3 in favour of acquittal this substantial weight of opinion in favour of the defendant ought to be accepted as an end to the prosecution. The proposal is not entirely satisfactory but it goes some way towards meeting the reservations of those who point to the cost of retrials caused by hung juries and also of those who object to the notion of conviction by majority.

Chapter 6

The Rise of the Magistracy

The magistracy once exercised considerable power when sitting with juries at Quarter Sessions but until the middle of the last century their summary jurisdiction was very limited. Up to that point the magistracy in its summary role was empowered to deal with very minor breaches of public order, for example game law offences, and certain quasi-criminal matters concerned with the regulation of the economy. This last feature reflects the fact that their prime function was that of local government, which then consisted of little more than the administration of the Poor Law, provision for proper roads, sanitation, the enforcement of public order, and securing compliance with the various directives emanating from central Government.

The role of the Justice of the Peace dates back to the fourteenth century, some 100 years after the beginning of the jury system. Although mocked (for example, Shakespeare's Justice Shallow) and occasionally reviled,[1] it has continually grown in strength. In the last two decades, aided by the Justices' Clerks Society, it has become a powerful semi-autonomous institution; in theory it is the child of the Lord Chancellor, in practice it is largely independent of him in daily affairs.

This amateur system of justice has always had some powerful friends: 'no part of the Christian world hath like office as justice of the peace if duly executed', said Coke;[2] but in retrospect it is surprising that it has survived to the present day, let alone become the corner-stone of the English legal system. It is particularly surprising since in the eighteenth century it had fallen into disrepute in developing urban areas. Corruption was common; the Middlesex

Bench being particularly notorious.[3] It was, in part, to counter this situation that the stipendiary magistracy came into existence in the middle of the eighteenth century.[4] Another reason was to deal expeditiously with the burgeoning case loads in the growing towns.

In the country the magistracy was composed solely of the landowning classes and the game laws were the means whereby they protected their sport (the often savage penalties used to enforce these laws were a source of much bitterness in rural England). It is therefore unsurprising that the magistracy was unpopular in country areas. Sidney and Beatrice Webb recorded that 'a farmer coursing hares on his own land with the permission of his own landlord was summoned by Lord Buckingham, the owner of the adjoining land'.[5] The luckless man asked for time to arrange legal representation and was refused. He was tried and convicted by the Duke in his own parlour and on the evidence of the Duke's own servant.

Nineteenth-century reforms

By the 1830s it was evident to many that this amateur and often arbitrary manner of administering justice was not fulfilling the needs of an increasingly complex society. A number of reforms were introduced to tackle the problems. The Municipal Corporations Act 1835 divorced the judicial functions of the magistracy from those relating to local government. Other necessary measures followed: the gradual introduction, over the next 30 years, of police forces throughout England and Wales, assisted the magistracy who, hitherto, had been front-line keepers of the peace and as such had incurred widespread unpopularity, particularly because of their use of *agents provocateurs*. This gradual establishment of the police force confined the magistracy more and more to the exercise of its judicial functions.

Useful though this reform was, it did bring problems in its wake. The principal one was the unclear relationship between the magistracy and the police, and it is one which has remained blurred in the minds of many to this day. At the end of the last century it was not unusual for colliery-owning magistrates to lead troops or the police against striking workers. This tendency to look at the forces of law and order as a private army of the landowning classes was never more evident than during the Featherstone riots during St Leger race week in 1893, when a number of striking miners were shot and killed by troops acting under the direction of local land and colliery owning magistrates. On this occasion the police were absent; they had been dispatched to keep order at the races.[6]

Much has been done since to erase this perception of overly close relations between the enforcement of public order and the functions of the judiciary but there is still more that could be done. Old lags still refer to magistrates' courts as police courts and the initials MP (Metropolitan Police) may be seen even now in the mosaics on the floors of some of the older Inner London courts. In the provinces the legend 'Police Court' still appears over some court entrances.

Other reforms followed in nineteenth-century England. An Act of 1847[7] enabled justices to try any child aged 14 or less for any offence of larceny (although the child's consent was still necessary). The purpose of the statute was to ensure a quick trial and avoid the child being held in custody for lengthy periods in the company of adult, and perhaps hardened, offenders. Another reform was a statute which set out basic rules of procedure to be followed by magistrates.[8] It is indicative of the informal and amateur nature of summary justice that it was necessary to include provisions requiring magistrates to sit in public and to allow an accused person the opportunity to be represented if he so wished. The establishment of this rudimentary procedure opened the way to a massive extension of summary jurisdiction. The Criminal Justice Act 1855 gave the magistrates increased powers to deal with adult offenders charged with larceny, although again, it was necessary for the defendants to consent to summary trial.

Clearly, the reforms were desirable. The 1855 Act, in particular, allowed defendants a choice of the venue for their trial. It must be remembered, however, that their role in the proceedings was limited. For example, they still could not give evidence on their own behalf. It must be said that the aims of the legislators were not wholly altruistic. The defendant may have had a quick disposal of his case by a tribunal whose powers of sentencing were strictly limited, but the quid pro quo for the State was an easing of the case load at Quarter Sessions and Assizes, with consequent financial savings.

The twentieth century

Further reforms followed piecemeal. One such was the Criminal Justice Act 1925 which added a further number of offences, formerly triable only on indictment, which could now be dealt with by magistrates (with the consent of the accused). The offences included actual bodily harm, malicious wounding, and attempted suicide. Additions to these cases came with the Administration of Justice Act 1962 (non-domestic breaking and entering, and any indecent assault upon an adult). The Theft Act 1968 added the burglary of a dwelling house (except where entry was obtained by force or deception).

The extent of these reforms reflected the increasing case-load of the higher courts and increasing confidence, by the executive at least, in the magistracy. Yet none of these reforms impinged on the right of the adult defendant to choose jury trial if he so wished. This much was expressly stated in the Streatfield Report.[9]

The James Committee Report 1975

The next step was brought about by the recommendations of the James Committee whose terms of reference were to 'consider within the existing legal framework what should be the distribution of criminal business between the Crown Court and Magistrates'.[10]

It was, at first sight, a fairly innocuous brief, but rather less so when the view of the then Home Secretary, Robert Carr, is considered. In reply to a 'planted' question in the House of Commons enquiring what proposals the government had for 'relieving the Crown Court of minor cases', the Home Secretary prefaced his announcement that the James Committee was to be established with the words: 'The Lord Chancellor and I are aware of the heavy pressure on, and delays in, the Crown Court, and of the widespread view that the law at present allows too many cases to go to trial there.'[11]

The opposite view, of course, was widely held, but the opinion of the Government was plain enough. Indeed it is difficult to avoid the conclusion that a proscription of the right to trial was an inevitable result of the setting up of the Committee. The political will in favour of a transfer of jurisdiction was evident. The terms of reference were loaded in favour of such a finding. And six of the 13-strong Committee were stipendiary magistrates, justices, or clerks to the justices.

Perhaps because of the strictures of the terms of reference there was only slight discussion of whether there were, in fact, too many cases going to the Crown Court rather than a factual analysis of the resources then available to try the case-load without undue delay. Similarly, there was little in the report of the alternatives to the transfer of jurisdiction to the magistrates. Those who thought the competence of the magistracy would have been a prime issue were to be disappointed. Although there was some discussion of the deficiencies of summary trial, and even minor criticisms,[12] competence was more or less taken for granted.

The report, within its terms of reference, was well researched and thought out. Many of its recommendations were later enacted, including the proposal in respect of advance disclosure, the system of classifying offences, and the transfer of cases to the sole jurisdiction of the magistracy. In this last respect the Committee was reviving a long-dormant trend.

The Committee's recommendations

In brief, the following offences were to be transferred to the sole jurisdiction of the magistrates:

1. Any offence of theft and any related offence of dishonesty where the value of the property which is the subject of the charge does not exceed £20. Any offence of theft from the person or any offence which was one of a series was excepted;
2. Any offence of criminal damage (not amounting to arson) where the value did not exceed £100;
3. Drink-drive offences;
4. Homosexual soliciting;
5. Using threatening, abusive, or insulting words and behaviour contrary to Section 5 of the Public Order Act 1936 and related offences;
6. Offences for which the maximum penalty on indictment is within the powers of the magistracy.

It was also proposed that the Home Secretary should have the power to increase the monetary limits in respect of theft and criminal damage, although only to keep pace with inflation.

Criminal Law Act 1977

Almost all these proposals were adopted by the Government and incorporated in the Criminal Law Act 1977. By way of contrast, one of the few proposals which offered significant advantage to the defendant – the proposals relating to advance disclosure of the prosecution's case before the defendant exercised his right of election – was not implemented for many years.

In some respects the Bill went further than the proposals of the

James Committee. For instance, the offence of assaulting a police officer in the execution of his duty was made into a purely summary offence, although conviction carries a substantial risk of an immediate prison sentence. It is a matter which usually depends wholly on police evidence; arguably a reason in itself for allowing a defendant the right to elect jury trial.

At one stage the Criminal Law Bill also included the Committee's most controversial suggestion that the defendants accused of so-called minor theft should no longer have the right to elect trial by jury. It was pointed out that the effects of a conviction for dishonesty could be ruinous and that only a defendant or his legal advisers could properly assess the impact and importance of such a conviction. The example of a bank manager charged with theft of a small sum of money was often cited as an example. Opposition in Parliament was such that the measure was withdrawn.

Other arguments were advanced against an extension of summary jurisdiction. The principal one – that jury trial offered a better standard of justice and a safeguard to the individual against the State – suffered a blow when the Government produced statistics to show that the acquittal rates before magistrates were slightly greater than those before juries.[13] These figures were advanced whilst the debate took place in Parliament, and although experienced criminal practitioners knew they flew in the face of reality, they could not be rebutted at that time.

Some years later the Home Secretary rather coyly admitted that 'statistics which indicated that acquittal rates in the magistrates' courts did not differ much from those in the Crown Court can no longer be regarded as valid'.[14] Subsequent research carried out by the Home Office has indicated that juries do acquit much more readily than magistrates.[15]

The plain and unavoidable conclusion is that Parliament was persuaded, in part at least, to transfer a host of offences to the sole jurisdiction of magistrates on the basis of statistics which proved to be completely misleading. Something of an irony can be detected here. The discredited statistics which suggested that magistrates acquitted at least as often as juries were used as a major argument in extending summary jurisdiction. On the other hand, recent research showing that juries acquit more readily has been used to suggest that many juries are incompetent, lawless, or both, and that they are therefore a poor alternative to trial by magistrates.

Recent developments

A small but indicative example of the trend towards trial by the magistracy is the High Court decision in the case of *Osaseri*.[16] It concerned
an allegation of assault under the Offences Against the Persons Act
1861, section 42, which had escaped the reclassification of offences
under the Criminal Law Act 1977. The question of whether such
an offence carried the right of trial by jury remained an open one,
until recently the High Court decided that the offence was a summary
one at the sole discretion of the justices. In other words, they could,
if they wished, decline jurisdiction but the choice was not open to
the defendant.

The Criminal Justice Act 1988 has effectively removed from the
jury the offence of criminal damage. The £100 limit below which
the offence of causing criminal damage was made a summary matter
by the Criminal Law Act 1977, was soon doubled and then redoubled.
It came as no surprise that the Criminal Justice Act 1988 section
38 has massively raised the threshold to £2,000 (the limit of the powers
of a magistrates' court to award compensation), at the same time
making common assault, driving whilst disqualified, and taking a
motor vehicle without the consent of the owner triable only in magistrates' courts. (One, perhaps unintentional, effect of raising the
threshold has been to stop one nefarious practice of prosecutors. In
recent years a number of police forces have stooped to fixing the
value of the damage caused below the then current limit, irrespective
of the actual amount of damage caused, so as to keep the cases before
magistrates.)

It cannot be long before Parliament is asked again to consider
the withdrawal of minor theft cases from the jury. On this occasion
they may accede to the suggestion, for it seems that a sizeable faction
within the Criminal Bar Association has been suggesting that the
theft of property valued at less than £250 should be triable only in
the magistrates' courts.[17] It is a point of view which has had broad
support from successive Lord Chancellors, the powerful Magistrates'
Association, and the Justices' Clerks Society.[18]

The present position

The rise of the lay magistracy since the early Victorian years has
been one of the more remarkable developments in our system of
criminal justice. There are now some 27,000 lay magistrates and,

sitting principally in London and such cities as Leeds, Cardiff, Liverpool and Birmingham, around 80 stipendiary and deputy stipendiary magistrates. They have power to deal with all summary cases and may, with the consent of the accused, deal with any 'either-way' case, that is one triable either summarily or on indictment. They do not have to accept jurisdiction for these cases even if both the prosecution and the defence ask them to do so. They have the power to impose a maximum of six months' imprisonment, or twelve months where the defendant has consented to be dealt with by them for two offences both of which are triable summarily or on indictment.

In the event of the magistrates thinking that their powers of sentence are insufficient, they still have the power to commit the accused to the Crown Court for sentence. They also consider as examining magistrates cases which are indictable only in order to decide whether there is a prima facie case on which to commit the defendant to stand his trial before a jury. Of all criminal business in England and Wales 97% is conducted before magistrates (who have also an extensive civil jurisdiction in such fields as child care, affiliation proceedings, matrimonial cases, and as licensing justices).

Conversely, the jury trial in criminal cases has undergone a relative decline, increasingly reserved for the most serious offences. The shift of jurisdiction towards the magistrates shows no signs of ceasing. There is, for instance, no general agreement on any set of principles which might determine whether an offence merits trial by judge and jury, other than the seriousness of the offence, which is measured out by a very broad rule of thumb.

Managing criminal business

The issue which has dominated the debate over the transfer of jurisdiction is the cost of the criminal justice system. Prominent amongst those favouring the extension of summary jurisdiction has been the administrative lobby. This includes the Home Office,[19] successive Lord Chancellors,[20] members of the judiciary,[21] the lay magistracy,[22] the Prosecuting Solicitors' Society,[23] and the Justices' Clerks Society;[24] all of whom have a vested interest in the expeditious disposal of criminal business and/or the aim of containing the cost of the system. Thus the membership of the James Committee reflected these interests, as did the subsequent report which, not surprisingly, proved to be a fairly clinical cost and efficiency study.

In the opposite camp are what might be termed the 'civil libertarians'; including the NCCL which has opposed rigorously any encroachment on the right to jury trial.[25] Regrettably the last 20 years have witnessed the development of a direct conflict of interest between the needs of the individual and those of the State, and it is fair to say that there has proved to be little middle ground between the protagonists.

The increasing volume of criminal business, the increasing length of trials involving juries, the extension of legal aid (at the Crown Court some 98% of defendants are legally aided), and the resulting cost to the taxpayer have been problems for many years, but it is only recently that attempts to resolve these issues have been made through restricting the right of the defendant to elect trial at the Crown Court.

Alternative solutions

It has long been recognised that if every defendant who could elect trial did so and entered a plea of not guilty, the system would break down within a matter of months if not weeks. That this has not happened is attributable, at least in part, to the efforts of those involved in the administration of justice to reduce the case-load to manageable proportions. The measures used have been a mixture of the carrot and the stick.

Pleas and plea bargaining
A plea of guilty at the magistrates' court has to the administration the advantage of a speedy and cheap conclusion to the case. From the defendant's point of view the knowledge that the bench has limited powers of punishment is an attraction. Again, he or she may wish the case to be heard as quickly as possible. The strain of waiting for trial at the Crown Court has often been cited as a reason for the suicide of television personality Lady Isobel Barnett, herself a one-time magistrate, who was eventually convicted of theft. It is an argument advanced, seemingly without self-interest, by those who would wish to restrict jury trial.

At the Crown Court the defendant who pleads guilty can expect a reduction in sentence as a matter of law.[26] It is therefore a powerful incentive to plead guilty particularly if there is a narrow margin in prospect between a custodial sentence and a non-custodial one.

Plea bargaining has always been a fact of life in our system of justice. It has been a matter of course for the police to prefer more serious charges in the expectation that the defendant will tender a plea to lesser charges in return for the major one being dropped. A common example of this has been the charge of conspiracy, used to persuade a defendant to plead to the substantive charges on the indictment; or simply the threat of a charge of conspiracy (triable only before a judge and jury) to procure a plea of guilty in the magistrates' court. There are, in fact, a number of variations on how such a bargain may be struck between prosecuting and defence lawyers, often with the active participation of the trial judge. After all, for both police and administration there is some truth in the maxim 'any conviction is better than no conviction'. It is a pragmatic approach to resolving disputes without the necessity of a trial. The results can be measured in court time saved and prosecution resources reallocated, although these criteria do not always operate in the interests of defendants.

What is also commonly called plea bargaining in the courts of England and Wales is more properly sentence bargaining. This practice has never had a respectable name: indeed it has been outlawed since the case of Turner.[27] It has, nevertheless, been a very common feature of our system and has made a significant contribution to the smooth running of our courts. The procedure, which involves the total co-operation of the trial judge, commences when the judge is approached by the defence (with the prosecution in attendance), and asked to indicate the length of the sentence, or whether an immediate custodial sentence will be imposed, should the defendant plead guilty. It relies on mutual trust between counsel and judge as well as defendant and counsel. There is a considerable body of anecdotal evidence that this practice is being revived in London, if not elsewhere, having lain dormant for almost 20 years.

Advance disclosure
The disclosure of the prosecution statements to the defendant prior to trial has long been recognised as a desirable principle in English law. In the past if the defendant elected trial on indictment, he was able to see at the committal proceedings the details of the case alleged against him. There was no such opportunity in cases contested in the magistrates' court even if the defendant had the right to elect trial by jury but chose not to exercise it. Where the defendant elected

trial by jury he was still not allowed to see the statements of the prosecution before he had committed himself one way or another, nor as a general rule, was he allowed to change his mind.

The James Committee was among the first to suggest that the prosecution be made to disclose its hand before the defendant was put to his election as to the venue of the trial. However, it was not until 1985 that the advance disclosure rules came into practice. It should be remembered that those cases which are triable summarily still do not entitle the defendant to see the evidence against him until the moment the witnesses give evidence. He is therefore at a significant disadvantage. In practice application may be made to the Crown Prosecution Service for copies of the statements of the witnesses for the prosecution but there is no obligation on the Service to disclose them. At present, because of lack of funds and manpower, the statements are rarely served.

Ironically, such evidence as there is suggests that the advance disclosure procedure is an effective means of persuading a defendant to plead guilty. John Baldwin's case study *Pre-Trial Justice* provides a common example of the process:

Defence Solicitor (at the outset of the pre-trial review): 'I want some ammunition ... what we really want, if you could supply it, such information about whether to lean on him. Have you lots of nice verbals?'

Prosecuting Solicitor: 'Right – I don't know about particularly nice verbals.' (He then reads out the statements of two police officers who saw a group of youths threatening to attack a man in the city centre. He gives the defence solicitor a copy of the defendant's statement made to the police and this strongly implicates him in the offence.)

Prosecuting Solicitor: 'I think that should give you some of the necessary information to go back to him ... Do you think you've now got sufficient to get a plea?'[28]

This kind of informal discussion has long been common between defence and prosecution solicitors. In the example above a number of consequences flowed from the supply of prosecution statements to the defence. Firstly, the defendant was to be advised, in strong terms and by his own solicitor, to plead guilty. Secondly, from the point of view of the court administrators it meant that court time which had been set aside could be redeployed. Thirdly, to the advantage of the prosecution, its own resources could be redeployed.

Costs

The award of costs in criminal cases is governed by the Prosecution of Offences Act 1985. Under the Act the prosecution may apply for costs against a convicted defendant. Indeed it is the policy of the Crown Prosecution Service to make such application at every reasonable opportunity. Equally, an acquitted defendant is entitled to his costs from the Treasury, from what is known as 'central funds'. On the face of it therefore, the Act is even-handed. However, costs in the Crown Court are invariably much higher than in the magistrates' court; the Act has created a provision which can be a positive disincentive to defendants electing trial by jury.

It may well be said that defendants who elect trial on indictment, with all the inherent expense, should bear a proportionate sum in costs if convicted; however, it is interesting to note that prior to the passing of the Act the costs of the prosecution of any indictable offence were usually asked for and paid out of Government funds irrespective of the verdict.[29]

The purpose of the Prosecution of Offences Act was to set up a national prosecution service, not to alter the distribution of business between the magistrates' and the Crown Court. (It is interesting to note that new provisions on costs went through Parliament without debate.)[30]

It is a matter of regret that this state of affairs has arisen. It is nonsense to speak of a right to trial by jury where a defendant's choice of trial venue is dictated by his means. It is now incumbent on defence lawyers to advise their clients that if they elect trial by jury and are convicted they run the risk of being ordered to pay substantial costs which may be out of proportion to the sentence imposed.

This combination of factors illustrates how the managerial priorities of those responsible for the smooth running of the system affect the manner in which justice is dispensed. They also show how the debate on the future of the criminal justice system has become dominated by considerations of cost and efficiency.

Limitations of summary trial

There has been little in the way of research on this aspect of the transfer of jurisdiction. Indeed, the argument in favour of summary trial has, for many years, been won by default. It is as though few people have been prepared openly to contemplate the implications of a finding which is unfavourable to summary trial.

Most people who become magistrates do so for the very best of reasons. All give up a good deal of time without any financial reward, and most apply themselves diligently and patiently to their work. There are, however, others who have become magistrates with at least half an eye on the resulting status of being 'one of Her Majesty's Justices of the Peace' and others who despite years on the bench have little comprehension as to procedure.

There are, in addition, certain features of summary trial which compare unfavourably with trial by jury. Some are of an intangible nature arising out of the methods of selecting candidates for the bench and which, consequently, are inherent in the distinct social and cultural attitudes and values of the lay magistracy.[31] There are also other tangible disadvantages to summary trial which tend to result from the way the court system is organised. We can usefully deal with these first.

The *voir dire*

Where it is argued that a confession made by an accused was obtained by oppression or that there is some other reason for rendering the confession unreliable, it is usual to hold a trial within a trial to establish whether to admit the confession in evidence. This is known as the *voir dire*.[32]

Since magistrates are judges of both law and fact they have to hear the alleged confession before ruling on its admissibility. The problem is, therefore, that even if the bench does rule the confession to be inadmissible they will certainly have difficulty in disregarding the excluded material when considering the remainder of the prosecution case. It is one of the mental hoops in the English legal system through which magistrates are expected to be able to leap without the slightest hesitation.

In the Crown Court, in such a case, the position is infinitely preferable. An application to have a confession ruled inadmissible is made to the trial judge in the absence of the jury. If the application succeeds then the jury will not hear any of the inadmissible evidence. It is a simple device which avoids any prejudice to the defendant. It is only possible because of the separate functions of judge and jury, and it is one which cannot be emulated in the lower court.

Cross-examination of a defendant as to previous convictions

Here there is an analogous situation. In specific circumstances where, for instance, the defendant has wrongly asserted his good character or impugned the character of a prosecution witness, the prosecution may be allowed to call evidence of the defendant's previous convictions or to cross-examine him about his character. To do this it is always necessary for the prosecution to apply for the leave of the court.

In the magistrates' court such an application is made to the bench. The drawback becomes immediately apparent: even if the application is unsuccessful the bench will know the defendant has something of a 'past', something to hide, and as such difficult to ignore. In the Crown Court, where the application is made to the judge in the absence of the jury, the problem does not arise.

Continuity

Jury trials are heard without interruption. Any summary trial lasting more than half a day runs the risk of being adjourned part-heard. Reconvening a lay bench on a date suitable to all parties invariably poses difficulties. It is not uncommon for a defendant to find that, at the reconvened hearing, the lawyer who appeared for him on one or more earlier occasions is now unavailable and a last minute substitute has been provided. The same state of affairs applies equally to the prosecution. It should be said that counsel and solicitors do make every effort to appear in part-heard cases when acting for the defence, though it seems they do not make the same effort when acting for the Crown.

The situation is still more unsatisfactory when all parties are unable to reconvene within weeks, or worse still when a further adjournment is necessary. These situations cause particular problems for the defence for their effect is to dull the impact of any inroads which may have been made into the prosecution case; this is particularly true where the credibility of witnesses is a prime issue.

Legal expertise

Whilst a jury will have the benefit of the directions and guidance of a professional judge, the lay magistracy frequently does not have a qualified lawyer to advise them. Very often the clerk who sits with them will not even have a law degree.

There is also the issue of advocacy. In magistrates' courts the standard of advocacy generally is not high. Usually, unless the case is one of importance or there is a member of chambers temporarily between Crown Court cases, only the young, inexperienced, and perhaps less able counsel appear in magistrates' courts. Similarly, many solicitors who appear are inexperienced or have no aptitude for advocacy or knowledge of the subtleties of the law. Thus, when the bench most needs help from the advocates there is often little available.

Sentencing

While newspaper reports of sentencing in rape cases might lead one to suppose otherwise, the professional judge at the Crown Court is trained to apply a considerable body of case law which means that, overall, sentencing in the Crown Court tends to be consistent throughout England and Wales. On the other hand there is evidence that sentencing varies considerably from one magistrates' court to another, from one bench to another in that court, and even, in straightforward matters during a morning's sitting, by the same bench. The imposition of custodial sentences may vary between 3% in one magistrates' court and 19% in another. The figures may, to a certain extent, reflect regional problems but they give rise to considerable concern.[33]

Once again the court is not helped by the lack of professional advice. And although magistrates are enjoined to undergo training sessions, visit penal institutions, and attend lectures it is usually the ones most in need of such guidance and training who are absentees.

Advance disclosure

We have already noted that advance disclosure is not available in cases triable only by magistrates. Since the work involved for the prosecution is usually a matter of photocopying a few pages of material it is a matter of great regret that the often inadequate and unrepresented defendant is put in the position of not knowing the case against him until the moment the witness steps into the box.

Case hardening

It is true to say that magistrates, like judges, become case hardened by their experiences. It may explain at least partially the belief held by practitioners that magistrates pay only lip service to the standard of proof. Juries, in general, come fresh to the criminal justice system.

They are directed to apply the high standard of proof which the law requires before conviction and, in general, they do so.

Legal aid

Whilst 98% of all defendants at the Crown Court are legally aided, research indicates that there are considerable variations in the willingness of different magistrates' courts to grant legal aid. In the 1960s, for example, at Great Marlborough Street magistrates court, the policy was never to grant legal aid in a case of shop-lifting. More recently, some courts will not grant legal aid until after the defendant has made his choice of mode of trial, whilst others will only grant legal aid for a plea in mitigation of sentence to be made, even if the defendant has contested the case. The Legal Action Group publishes annually a table of statistics showing where in London and the rest of the country legal aid is likely to be granted or refused. There are very wide variations in the figures. It is noticeable that the courts which operate what practitioners regard as a generally repressive attitude to defendants are usually amongst those who are most likely to refuse legal aid.

Selection composition and the outlook of magistrates and their courts

It is open for any adult individual to apply to be a magistrate, although, in fact, candidates tend to find their way on to a bench by way of a recommendation from an organisation or group active in the community: a political party, trade union, or charity, for example. Alternatively it is quite common for serving magistrates to put forward for consideration the name of a business colleague or other acquaintance.

Potential magistrates are not necessarily disqualified because of a past conviction. Lord Hailsham himself thought that knocking off a policeman's helmet whilst at university need not be an absolute bar. (Whether knocking off that helmet in a demonstration outside the American Embassy would be viewed in a similar light is more doubtful.)

Applications are sifted by Advisory Committees or Area Sub-Committees. The names of suitable candidates are then forwarded to the Lord Chancellor. It seems rare for him to refuse on the grounds of suitability a nomination from an Advisory Committee. There appear to be two principles upon which the selection process is based.

The first is that the candidate should be suitable to hold office and be recognised locally to be so fitted. Such a candidate, in Lord Hailsham's words, would be 'properly motivated to do justice between man and man and the State and the individual'.[34] Questions put to a candidate would appear to be those designed to test reactions to current moral problems such as 'What action would you take if, on your return home, you found your son and his friend smoking cannabis in the kitchen?' The second principle is that any given bench should reflect a cross-section of society in the hope of cancelling out the prejudices of individuals and remaining in touch with local people and problems. (This second principle is the product of a not too distant era when appointments to the bench were often a reward for political services to the Government.) A candidate will more often be turned down or stayed in the interests of establishing or preserving a balance within a particular bench. This is often achieved by no more sophisticated a method than ensuring the adequate representation on the bench of each political party.

Membership of Advisory Committees has been the subject of masonic-like secrecy, so as to protect the members from being canvassed by aspiring candidates. (Parenthetically, it might be thought that they should be more open so that canvassing may disqualify.) The fear of canvassing by aspirants is understandable but the rigidity with which the rule has been enforced has contributed to a system of selection which has been described as 'probably the most secretive administrative organisation in Britain'.[35] Secret it undoubtedly is and therefore unaccountable to the public. The present Lord Chancellor, Lord Mackay, has indicated that the process may be subject to review.

Research by Burney, and also by King and May, has unearthed sufficient information to make a number of general observations on the composition of Advisory Committees:

1. The vast majority of those who serve on Advisory Committees are serving or retired magistrates;
2. Clerks to Justices and Chairmen of the Bench tend to serve as Secretary and Chairman representing their local committee;
3. The actual process of selection tends to be carried out by a small number of individuals within those committees.

The consequences of such a selection process are obvious. Those selected tend to be of the same background and outlook as their selectors and are unlikely to rock the boat. We have encountered one female applicant who was asked by one Advisory Committee

'And how do you think your liberal attitudes will help us in our deliberations?' Another classic, and widely quoted, example of this tendency is the survey of the Rochdale bench in the 1970s which showed that 29 out of 43 magistrates were either Masons, Rotarians, or both.[36]

Research also indicates that magistrates tend to be white, middle-aged, and middle-class. In general, their politics reflect this as does their working background; lay magistrates are mainly drawn from professional and managerial classes. Few are below the age of 30, and representatives of the black and other ethnic minority communities are significantly under-represented on the bench.

It is said that the cause of such discrepancies is simply that not enough suitable candidates are coming forward who are from black, Asian, young, or working-class backgrounds. This may be a contributory factor but there are other causes. For instance it is disturbing to note that King and May's study of the selection process concludes: 'There is evidence of racial prejudice amongst some members of the Lord Chancellor's Advisory Committees' and that 'there is some evidence of indirect discrimination in the procedure adopted and criteria applied.'[37]

Despite the real efforts of successive Lord Chancellors the magistracy is not at all representative of the community at large. Many magistrates have little in common with those classes of people who most commonly come before the courts; the young, unemployed, perhaps inarticulate and with a disproportionate number drawn from ethnic minorities.

If this was the worst that could be said then these imbalances in composition would be of little consequence; but clearly the attitudes of the magistracy are reflected in the decision making process. Two areas are worthy of consideration. First, race and secondly a perception held by many magistrates of their role in the criminal justice system, particularly in relation to the police.

Magistrates and race
As we have said, King and May's research indicates that racism is an operative factor in the selection of magistrates and that the vast majority of those involved in the selection process are themselves serving or retired magistrates. If the research is correct, and we cannot find that it has effectively been challenged, it is reasonable to assume that racism may be a factor in the trial process itself. Is there any

other evidence to support this disturbing picture? The answer must be a qualified 'yes'. A number of black magistrates interviewed by King and May expressed the view that many of their white colleagues were racist to one degree or another. Other evidence on this point is divided and does not all relate directly to the involvement of the magistracy. A recent study of sentencing in the Crown Court disclosed no relation between sentencing and race.[38] On the other hand a Home Office study has indicated that arrests and convictions in London include a disproportionately high number of black people. This is not itself conclusive proof of racism operating in the trial process for there are a number of ways in which these statistics can be interpreted and therefore they should be treated with caution.

None the less, there is a recent report by the National Association for the Care and Resettlement of Offenders (NACRO) which cites evidence (some empirical and some anecdotal) that black defendants fare badly by comparison with white defendants of a similar background. Black defendants are more likely to be stopped and searched, more likely to be arrested, less likely to be granted bail, and more likely to receive a custodial sentence. The conclusion of the NACRO report is that there is at least 'cause for concern'. That is a view with which many practitioners will agree.

The incidence of racism in the criminal process is impossible to assess with any degree of confidence. A good deal of the research available is unsatisfactory and inconclusive. On the basis of King and May's study, it can tentatively be said that an uncertain number of justices consciously or unconsciously harbour racist views. What is more certain is that a significant proportion of black people share this perception. Consequently, until racism is eliminated and the magistracy is able to inspire confidence generally, then this will continue to be yet another reason why many defendants shun trial before the justices.

In passing it should be noted that there is no research into the incidence of racism in juries. Section 8 of the Contempt of Court Act 1981 has put paid to direct research into the functioning of the jury. Common sense dictates that it must occur. However, the effect of one racist magistrate on a bench of two or three will have a telling effect. The views of a single racist juror should hopefully be absorbed within the random group of twelve. Certainly in today's climate any juror expressing an overtly racist attitude to a defendant would be likely to receive short shrift from his fellow jurors.

Magistrates and police

The view of many practitioners, and certainly many defendants, is that many magistrates unduly favour the police, that they are uncritical of officers and accept too readily the prosecution's evidence. It is a view that can all too easily be justified by spending a morning or two in any busy magistrates' court. This bias in favour of the prosecution may be explained in a number of ways, for example, by case hardening syndrome. There is, after all, a limit to the number of times anyone can be expected to believe that goods were purchased in a public house without a receipt, from a red-headed man known only as 'Scotty'. There is also the class make up of the magistracy. Many could not even imagine the infra-structure of a community in which goods are quite legitimately sold at knock-down prices without receipts in public houses and on shop and factory floors.

Finally, there is the perception of many magistrates of their own role in the criminal justice system; the remains of an historical legacy of an age when magistrates enjoyed almost a master/servant relationship with the police, which to some extent still flourishes. The magistrate is called 'Sir' or 'Madam' by the officer both in or out of court. It is not so long ago that an officer parked their cars and gave advice how best to deal with the minor scrapes in which they found themselves. An officer often provided tea for the justices and was on hand to make life more comfortable for them whilst they were at court; they were even known to provide bodyguard services. The police officer is still a partially hidden Figaro figure to the magistrates' Count and Countess.

In recent years efforts have been made to distance the magistracy from the police. We have commented upon the floor mosaics, but these are disappearing, as is the legend 'Police Court' on the front of the building. Since the Prosecution of Offences Act 1985 police officers no longer prosecute cases before the justices. Except in the busiest of courts the once highly visible role of the court officer has vanished. The reforms have not been merely procedural. They have reflected a laudable desire to distance the magistracy from the police in the eyes of the public. Nevertheless, the overly close relation between magistracy and police has been a substantial contributory factor in the distrust shown towards the magistracy by the working class.

It is doubtful whether this 'us and them' syndrome can be eradicated. This is a problem in itself, let alone the distinct belief that the magistracy is but the executive arm of the police. Whilst efforts are made to eliminate the appearance of partiality in favour of the police there is evidence that bias in their favour still exists amongst magistrates. Strong links remain between police and magistracy. They share a prime function, broadly expressed as 'keeping the peace'. Magistrates are in a position to observe the police carrying out a thoroughly difficult, unpleasant, and sometimes dangerous job. Not unnaturally many magistrates feel a degree of sympathy for the officers who come before them. In some instances a rapport springs up between a magistrate and an officer who appears regularly in one court. It is a fact which the James Committee noted with disapproval in a paragraph headed 'The apparent relationship between the bench and prosecutor.'

Examples of this phenomenon abound. There is for instance a chairman of a bench who announced the court's decision to convict in these words: 'Quite the most unpleasant cases that we have to decide are those where the evidence is a direct conflict between a police officer and a member of the public. My principle in such cases has always been to believe the evidence of the police officer, and therefore we find the case proved.'[39] This is some confirmation of a widely-held belief that the burden of proof is often reversed in the lower courts. In this case there was obviously the clearest possible failure on the part of the bench to carry out the most simple and basic judicial function; to weigh up the evidence and decide the case accordingly. It is a matter of speculation how many other lay magistrates share such a perception of their role in our system of criminal justice, but are rather more discreet.

That the example is not isolated is clear from a *cri de coeur* to *The Magistrate*, the justices' trade paper, in which a lay justice enquired: 'Is it our policy always to believe police evidence? Is it our position that no defendant can ever succeed in a defence the main basis of which is that the account of the incident given by the police is incorrect?'[40] Reading between the lines it is easy to see an ideological dispute which has arisen, one on which expert advice – other than that of the clerk – is sought. Yet another example along the same lines is quoted by Burney: 'I honestly don't think I've ever found a policeman who exaggerated his case or has been too tough.'[41]

In recent years one of the incidents for which a bench should feel collective shame became known as the Oxfraud Incident. In September 1982 Oxford police conducted an operation to net those suspected of obtaining DHSS benefits by deception. A temporary DHSS office was erected in the grounds of a school to facilitate 'the sting'. All claimants, totalling some 300, who entered were arrested. It must have been known that many innocents would be caught in the trap; and indeed some 133 of those seized were eventually released without charge. Roger Smith described what happened to the remainder when they went to court: 'Oxford magistrates sitting two to a bench in five courts processed the accused from 3 p.m. onwards sitting until about 11 p.m. Local solicitors and probation officers were not informed . . .'[42]

The remainder of the article is a sorry tale of men remanded in custody without representation, given prison sentences, and generally denied even the illusion of justice. Smith concluded that, at least initially, the courts appeared 'to allow themselves to be caught up in the drama of a mass police operation. In doing so they failed to maintain both their independence and their role as dispensers of individualised justice.' It is little comfort to say that with the arrival of the Crown Prosecution Service and the provisions of advance disclosure a recurrence is less likely.

Other examples of the behaviour of benches reflect an ill-disguised desire to convict in cases arising out of political or industrial unrest. Notable examples were apparent during the Grunwick dispute,[43] the Southall disturbances,[44] the National Graphical Association dispute,[45] and the miners' strike of 1984. In the trials associated with the miners' strike efforts were made by the majority of magistrates to be fair, but the performance of some benches left many sections of the community harbouring a keenly felt sense of injustice.

A feature of the cases which followed the Southall disturbances was the evident preference of the prosecution for summary trial. Most defendants were charged with summary offences, while those charged with offences which carried the right of trial by jury found that these charges were later substituted for similar offences triable only in the magistrates' court. The confidence of the police in summary trial was reflected in the fact that 'the prosecution manipulated the charges so as to avoid jury trial in as many cases as possible; and as it happened, all but six of the 342 accused were tried summarily.'[46]

This strong preference for summary trial, exhibited by the prosecution in the Southall cases, has been a feature of the prosecution of offences arising out of subsequent incidents of large-scale public disorder. Some prosecutors have the gall to suggest they are doing the defence a favour by substituting summary charges for indictable ones. Their argument is that they are removing the defendant from the peril of a longer sentence on conviction at the Crown Court. In reality they are seeking a territorial advantage for themselves. A classic example of this conduct is the substitution of a charge of assault on a police officer in the execution of his duty (summary only) in place of an assault causing actual bodily harm (triable either way).

The tendency of many magistrates to give preference to police evidence is also reflected in the statistics which indicate that juries acquit more readily than magistrates. These statistics are capable of a number of interpretations, but generally speaking most practitioners and most members of the judiciary feel that juries exercise their duties thoughtfully and conscientiously, exhibiting a healthy degree of independence and a readiness to apply to an exacting degree the standard of proof required by law.

The obverse of the independence of juries is the reliance the magistracy places on police evidence. Research shows that this reliance is often misplaced: police officers are sometimes mistaken; police officers do sometimes lie. That was the reluctant view of the Royal Commission on the Police which, in 1962, reported having received evidence from, amongst others, the Law Society and the Bow Group which: 'accused the police of stooping to the use of undesirable means of obtaining statements and occasionally giving perjured evidence'.[47]

The position today is no better and may, perhaps, be worse. There are, of course, no statistics available on the incidence of perjury amongst police officers. Nevertheless one survey tentatively suggested that police perjury may occur in three out of every ten trials in London.[48] The problem may not be confined to London. In July 1989 it was revealed that the West Midlands Serious Crimes Squad was being dispersed after several prosecutions in court had come to grief amidst allegations of police corruption. At the time of writing a number of officers have been disciplined and criminal prosecutions are pending against others. There have also been allegations that efforts have been made to suborn the enquiry. These findings are extremely disturbing and make it necessary to look for alternatives to the progressive extension of summary justice.

Alternatives to an extension of summary jurisdiction

The fundamental conclusion of the James Committee was that 'the Crown Court has been subject to increasing pressure of criminal business, with which it has been able to keep pace only as a result of large increases in the number of judges and staff and in the provision of court accommodation. Such increases cannot be progressively maintained.'[49]

Since then there has been another upsurge in the number of cases committed to the Crown Court. The only alternative, the argument runs, is a further proscription of the right to jury trial. This argument is flawed for a number of reasons. Firstly, not everyone accepts that cost and efficiency ought to be the prime considerations in deciding what offences should have the right of jury trial. There are also the problems concerned with expanding the magistracy sufficiently to cope with the increased work-load. Not only must there be an adequate number of magistrates of ability who can devote sufficient time to the task, but there must be a sufficient number of court clerks of the requisite calibre, not to mention the physical space needed to absorb the additional work. Already there are delays of a year or more between arrest and sentence in cases which are contested in magistrates' courts. Once justice was swift, if not certain. Now it can claim to be neither; if more cases are loaded onto the shoulders of the magistrates from the Crown Court overspill the position will deteriorate further.

The reasons for delays at the Crown Court are numerous. Some defendants elect trial at the Crown Court merely to buy time before their inevitable plea of guilty; in other cases there is insufficient preparation before an election is made, and so the case is committed unnecessarily to the Crown Court because the defence lawyers do not seek an old-style committal where the evidence may be challenged. The Crown Prosecution Service may fail to weed out weak cases at an early stage; while another cause of delay may be the reluctance of the magistracy to take a robust view and rule there is no case to answer. At the Crown Court inexperienced and sometimes inept counsel may prolong trials unnecessarily, and judges with little prior experience in criminal cases (sometimes chosen for the job because of their connections rather than their ability) do not have the necessary control of the case to stop them. None of these are reasons why defendants should be denied the right to jury trial. These defects and resulting delays might be eliminated by better training and education of both lawyers and the magistracy, but to do so will take time.

There remains the problem of an increased number of appeals

against decisions by the magistracy if their jurisdiction is enlarged. At the present time appeals to the Crown Court are by way of rehearing without a jury and are as of right. It is highly likely that dissatisfied defendants will appeal in greater numbers, clogging up the Crown Court lists and therefore partially defeating the object of the exercise. Until the magistracy can be seen and, more importantly, be believed by court users to provide even-handed justice then it is likely that the public (if not the politicians) will reject any additional extension of their jurisdiction.

Chapter 7

The Roskill Fraud Trials Committee Report

The majority of the Roskill Committee's recommendations have been adopted by the Government. However, the proposal to do away with juries in complex fraud trials was shelved after strong opposition in Parliament. Most informed observers believe that the proposal to abolish will be reinstated when the political climate is more favourable. This will very likely come about within the lifetime of the present administration with its all-pervading fascination with cost and efficiency. It is therefore appropriate to consider now the Roskill proposal in some detail.

The terms of reference of the Roskill Committee on fraud trials were apparently limited 'to consider in what ways the conduct of criminal proceedings in England and Wales arising from fraud can be improved and to consider what changes in existing law and procedure would be desirable to secure the just, expeditious, and economical disposal of such proceedings'.[1] It is revealing to note that the main reason why the Roskill Committee was set up was 'in response to growing public concern at the effectiveness of present methods of combating serious commercial fraud'.[2] In non-specific terms it was said that there was disquiet over an apparent failure by the Director of Public Prosecutions (DPP) to detect large-scale fraud and prosecute it to conviction. It should be noted that the Committee's chairman, Lord Roskill, was already on record as favouring the abolition of juries in cases of complex fraud citing as a reason for their disbandment the 'appalling waste' of public funds.[3] In these circumstances the Committee's recommendation to abolish jury trial was hardly surprising.

In considering its remit the Committee ranged far and wide over the jury system looking at such diverse aspects as the composition of juries, selection from the electoral role, age limits, literacy requirements, disqualifications, challenge, stand-by, and stand-by jurors, as well as the alternatives to jury trial. Additionally, the Committee took the opportunity to look at the jury systems in Hong Kong, America, New Zealand, Scotland, and six other jurisdictions.[4] In its report in 1986 the Committee made a number of proposals: 112 in all, of which 27 related specifically to the jury.[5]

The proposals for reform were comprehensive, covering every stage of the prosecution process from detection and investigation to the trial process itself. There were also proposals dealing with reforms of the law of evidence and trial procedure. Significantly, the Committee made it clear that its proposals need not be confined to fraud cases.[6] We, of course, are principally concerned with the proposals relating to trial procedure and the role of the jury.

Recommendations on trial procedure

It is not our task to describe in detail the inefficiencies and other problems which crop up time and again in the preparation of cases in the Crown Court, though they are many. Briefly, though, they include inadequate preparation by solicitors (partly because of restrictions on the defence obtaining expert advice at an early stage in the proceedings). There are also difficulties in instructing experienced counsel, who, because of the vagaries of the listing process at the Crown Court, may not be available for the trial. Another factor is the system under which the trial judge may not know he is taking a complicated case until very shortly before the hearing.

This last factor arises because traditionally there has been no supervision of cases once they are committed from the magistrates' court. This has a number of other consequences: arguments over admissibility of evidence, challenges to counts on the indictment, and other such matters must all be thrashed out when the trial actually commences, rather than having the case knocked into shape before the first day of the trial. In complicated commercial fraud cases there has been less returning of briefs. There are two reasons for this. Firstly, because the barrister's clerk is anxious to see his counsel involved in a long and therefore well-paid case; secondly, because this sort of case is usually the subject of a fixture, unlike other cases, which come into a warned list and may or may not be heard within the period of that warning.

With these and other problems in mind the Roskill Committee recommended more frequent use of a pre-trial review and that the same judge should preside at every stage after committal (a concept almost unknown in English criminal cases). It also suggested scheduling cases so that the judge has adequate time for preparation, again a procedure not common in the English courts.

With a view to simplifying and cutting down the length of trials the Roskill Committee made a number of proposals, notably the supply by the prosecution of an outline of the allegations and evidence proposed to be brought in support. The Committee also envisaged summaries, timetables, graphs to be agreed, and preliminary points of law to be argued before the empanelment of the jury.

There were also recommendations about the composition of the jury in simple fraud cases including:

1. The upper and lower age limits for jury service (18 and 65) should remain unchanged.

2. No one should sit on a jury in a fraud case who cannot read, write, speak, and understand English without difficulty.

3. The rules relating to the disqualification of persons from jury service should be reviewed in relation to the jury system as a whole, with a view to seeing whether and how far the disqualifications should be extended in scope.

4. The defendant's right of peremptory challenge of jurors and the prosecution's right to 'stand-by for the Crown' in any fraud trial should be abolished.

5. The prosecution and the defence should only be allowed to challenge jurors for cause in accordance with existing principles.

6. The determination of the validity of a challenge for cause should, if the judge so orders, be heard in chambers.

It might be thought that the totality of these proposals (some of which have already been implemented) would be sufficient in themselves, but instead of considering how these would operate and keeping more drastic measures in reserve (what Harding[7] describes as a fall back position), the Committee went on to make its most far-reaching and controversial recommendation: 'For complex fraud trials falling within certain guidelines, trial by a judge and two lay members should replace trial by judge and jury.'

The next 16 proposals dealt with the establishment and running of the 'Fraud Trials Tribunal' (the FTT), composed of a judge and two lay assessors. The Committee also proposed a right, of either prosecution or defence, to request that a case be heard by the FTT by way of application to a High Court judge, with an automatic right of appeal against a decision to the Court of Appeal.

The lay members of the tribunal would be vetted to ensure that neither had an extreme view and that they had sufficient business experience to comprehend the complex dealings with which they would be faced. The verdict was, if necessary, to be by a bare majority, and any dissenting opinion would not be disclosed. There would be a written or oral judgement. The judge alone would be responsible for matters of law and of sentence. It was the Committee's estimate that there would only be a few dozen of these cases annually.

At first sight the proposal to abolish the jury may not seem objectionable. The number of cases involved would be small compared with the number of jury trials annually. The total would probably be half the number of cases heard in a single court-room at the Central Criminal Court in any year. Under the new proposals there would be considerable financial savings in copying documents. Lengthy explanations which have at present to be made to the jury would be obviated, as would the need for a summing up by the trial judge.

The argument for the abolition of the jury in such cases effectively boiled down to a single point. Though bolstered by references to cost and the disruption of a juror's life during the time taken to try the case, it can be reduced to the phrase used by the Committee 'the limits of comprehension'.[8] In fact, however, the Committee was unable to point to any accurate evidence to prove there had been a higher proportion of acquittals or convictions in complex fraud cases than in simpler fraud cases or indeed other criminal cases overall. The Committee concluded: 'Nevertheless, we do not find trial by a random jury a satisfactory way of achieving justice in cases as long and complex as we have described. We believe that many jurors are out of their depth. The breadth of experience of these cases of many of our witnesses leads us to accept their evidence.'[9]

The recommendation to abolish the jury can be explained, at least in part, by the decision of the Director of Public Prosecutions not to prosecute in one particular major fraud case because a jury could not be expected to understand the allegations. The Committee reported that: 'We were told that this was rarely the sole reason, but that it was sometimes a major contributory factor in deciding not to proceed with a prosecution. We also had evidence that the difficulty of presenting a complex case often resulted in a decision to opt for less serious charges than the offences warranted.'[10] However, Walter Merricks' analysis* of the 179 fraud cases referred to the DPP in 1983 disclosed only one which was not prosecuted due to complexity.[11]

The Committee also cited the 'promptings of common sense' as a factor in their conclusion that many jurors were out of their depth. Though this may be superficially attractive it is poor evidence on which to abolish a constitutional right. It does not assist in identifying the scale of the problem (if there is one), nor does it assist in identifying alternative reforms short of abolition. In his dissenting opinion Walter Merricks noted that 'The great majority of those who gave written or oral evidence to the Committee were against the proposal' (to abolish).

The limits of comprehension argument was developed further by the Committee. As part of their remit they had commissioned a research unit at Cambridge to undertake four studies into aspects of jurors' comprehension. These were carried out by the unit with the assistance of volunteers sitting as mock jurors. The results do not tell us much more than we already know – that people have difficulty in absorbing complex information. It may be that the real value of such studies lies in identifying methods of improving the communication of complex material to jurors.

Criticisms of the proposals for the abolition of the jury

We do not blindly uphold the right to jury trial for all offences. We are open to persuasion that complex fraud trials might be a necessary exception to the rule that all serious cases ought to attract a right to elect trial by one's peers. However, the evidence advanced so far does not suggest that the interests of justice make such a reform necessary. Criticisms of the Roskill proposal can be reduced to three simple arguments: the first is that the Committee has failed to prove the case for abolition; the second is what one might describe as the 'thin end of the wedge argument', no less valid for being clichéd; the third relates to perceptions of the quality of justice that would flow from the setting up of the FTT.

* Committee Member Walter Merricks wrote a lengthy note of dissent to the Committee's Report.

Not proven

Because jury trial has attained the status of a constitutional right the onus of proving that it is necessary to withdraw that right must lie squarely on those who seek to restrict the right to trial. The evidence upon which the Roskill proposal was based was thin. It caused Louis Blom Cooper to write: 'The great majority of those who gave written or oral evidence to the committee – judges, barristers, solicitors, and the police – were against the proposal,' and that the Committee's report was 'deafeningly silent on this body of opinion'.[12] It is to the great credit of Walter Merricks that he provided a note of dissent to the Committee's proposal. At best it can be said that the Committee's findings amount simply to the 'promptings of common sense', and some mock jury research. The Committee produced no reliable evidence to show that juries were not fulfilling their proper functions. In this respect the Committee admitted that its work was hampered by the Contempt of Court Act 1981 Section 8, which prohibits the interviewing of jurors (the best source of evidence).

So far as the Cambridge research project is concerned the report accepts that it may well have suffered from the traditional problems associated with mock juries. Divided into four sections, the research considers the use of glossaries, presenting numerical information, concentration difficulties, and improving jurors' understanding. The study accepts its own limitations: 'The first concerns its adequacy as a simulation of a real trial ... It is not clear, however, how to overcome this difficulty without a full-scale trial simulation.'[13]

The wedge

Juries are called upon regularly to deal with complex scientific or forensic evidence. If fraud trials are to be removed from juries on the grounds of complexity then the way is open for the removal of jury trial in other cases, where, for instance, there is complex forensic evidence to be considered. In this respect it is highly significant that the Committee concluded that 'if our recommendations are adopted in fraud cases, it would seem logical for some of them to apply in all criminal cases.'[14]

The Committee's view was that society accepts many other forms of legal tribunal such as the lay and stipendiary magistrate, and that therefore the jury is not sacrosanct. The Committee believed that jury trial was the exception rather than the rule. But defenders of the jury trial have always argued that it should be retained for serious criminal cases and each derogation from the right of jury trial has been fiercely defended. The Committee, however, launched its own pre-emptive strike in an effort to dispose of 'the thin end of the wedge' argument: 'If the random and unqualified tribunal is a bastion of freedom, then the damage has already been done.'[15] In response one might say that merely because some damage has already been done is not a good argument for inflicting yet more damage.

The wedge argument is not, of course, particularly meritorious in itself. Suffice to say that the Roskill proposal to abolish juries in complex fraud trials might have attracted much more support if it did not smack of an insidious attack on the jury system itself.

Perceptions of justice

Differing treatment of differing cases will lead to the appearance of inequality amongst defendants and the impression that if a case is so serious and difficult that it is beyond a jury's comprehension, then the defendant must be guilty; any subsequent acquittal may then have the smell, in the nostrils of the public, of the old-boy network.

Set against that the FTT, as with any other legal tribunal sitting continually, will develop a case-hardened built-in bias towards the prosecution and therefore towards a conviction. (It must not be forgotten that the apparent failure of the prosecution authorities to produce convictions in complicated fraud cases was a prime reason for setting up the Roskill Committee.)

Removing the jury (the only lay element in the trial process) is likely to result in the professionals, the lawyers, and accountants, swamping the trial with professional jargon. As a result the necessity for the prosecution to explain in simple and understandable language why it says the defendant has committed a crime will be lost. It is an aspect of justice being seen to be done. An example of this is provided by the non-jury Diplock courts in Northern Ireland. Messrs Boyle, Hadden, and Hillyard observe that these trials can sometimes 'develop into a discussion between the judge and the lawyers of procedures and technicalities which lay observers, or a jury if there were one, would have some difficulty in following'.[16]

A further criticism has been made by Walter Merricks, who has pointed out that written judgements will have to be produced many of which are bound to be critical of defendants even if they are eventually acquitted. There will doubtless also be numerous comments adverse to prosecution witnesses, yet those witnesses will have no opportunity to correct or explain the comments.

An excellent illustration of this problem concerned the late George Wigg. He was accused of a public order offence, in effect, accosting women in Mayfair. The case was triable only summarily and the magistrate acquitted him. Unfortunately he thought to give a short judgement and said that he accepted the truth of the police evidence – which had been heavily challenged – but did not think that in law it established the case against the defendant. Wigg therefore had the worst of all worlds. He was branded both a liar and an importuner of women. He had no way in which to challenge the verdict. The introduction of the FTT system would, over the years, increase the number of incidents such as this.

The operation of the FTT would inevitably produce verdicts by a 2–1 majority. It might be said that this is a daily occurrence in the magistrates' courts, but there the penalties on conviction are strictly limited. In the Criminal Justice Act 1987 the penalties for conspiracy to defraud are set at a maximum of ten years' imprisonment – a far cry from the rarely exercised twelve months' imprisonment available to magistrates.

It should be said, finally, that one of the less well-known proposals of the Roskill Committee is that the lay assessors for any given trial would be chosen by the Lord Chancellor in consultation with the trial judge.[17] This proposal would inevitably increase the possibility of abuse and ample scope for allegations of corruption.

The way ahead

Many of Lord Roskill's recommendations (to which we do not dissent) have been adopted in the Criminal Justice Act 1988. Arguably, the Government has adopted a prudent and sensible course in not implementing the proposal to abolish jury trial although we have already indicated that this measure has not been ruled out if the lesser proposals which fall short of abolition are found to be lacking.

Surprisingly, there has been no indication that research is to be carried out in order to assess the efficacy of the new reforms. If there is to be no inquiry it is difficult to see how any reliable evidence can be obtained to substantiate any further proposed changes in this direction.

Conclusions

In the absence of direct evidence it must be accepted, as a matter of common sense, that the system of the random selection of juries means that many jurors will be unable to comprehend the issues they hear. This is an argument for ensuring jurors are literate and improving the techniques of explaining in lay terms what is said against defendants. The Roskill Committee demonstrated just how the techniques of defrauders have improved over the years. All the more reason for prosecution and courts to improve their techniques in explaining and exposing these frauds. The old Salvation Army motto that the devil should not have a monopoly on all the good tunes applies equally in fraud trials.

At present there is no evidence whatsoever that juries in these cases are coming to conclusions unsupported by the evidence or that acquittal and conviction rates differ from those in any other category of case. Walter Merricks pointed out that 'most judges and lawyers who made submissions thought that juries mostly reached the right result or at least an understandable result'. What, therefore, is to be gained by the abolition of the jury for the type of complex fraud trials envisaged by the Committee? The answer is that every year a mere half-dozen defrauders will be prosecuted, not necessarily to conviction.

The danger is that if the FTT were to become a part of the criminal process it would only be a short step away from the removal of the jury in, say, a complicated drug smuggling case. Indeed the Roskill Committee was quite open in its view that 'we have not proposed changes in law and procedure which we were not prepared to see applied to other types of criminal cases'.

We favour a number of alternative proposals, notably Merricks' suggested creation of summary trip-wire offences, together with a special court of summary jurisdiction and deterrent sentences of imprisonment for defrauders. We also suggest the development of the challenge for cause (which we discussed in Chapter 4) as one means of ensuring that jurors are capable of handling the particular case to which they are assigned. A special jury would be a less desirable alternative – though preferable to outright abolition. There is also the option of jury waiver which operates in many states of America. It is possible, however, that this option would set an undesirable precedent; given the current debate over juror comprehension, failure to exercise waiver might well attract an adverse inference.

Finally, we suggest that it would be particularly apposite in the case of complex fraud trials to commission academic research with a view to establishing the efficacy of the Roskill proposals which have already been implemented, and attempting to identify better methods of communicating complicated and voluminous evidence to jurors.

Chapter 8

The Suspension of Jury Trial in Northern Ireland

Civil rights and civil disorder

It is difficult to pinpoint the moment of conception of the non-jury criminal trial in Northern Ireland. Certainly, it has been employed frequently at different times in Ireland's troubled history. But so far as the non-jury Diplock Courts are concerned October 5, 1968 may well prove to be as good a date as any. On that day, only a few years after the Sharpeville massacre in South Africa and the Freedom Ride through the southern states of America, a civil rights march took place in Derry, Northern Ireland. The marchers followed the (hardly radical) banner of One Man – One Vote.[1] They were drawn mainly from the disadvantaged Catholic population. Like many of the demonstrations of that era it began as a peaceful and orderly event and ended in bloody violence and widespread public disorder. For most people outside Northern Ireland this incident marked the beginning of the 'Troubles', but the roots of civil disorder had been sown many years previously. Most political analysts agree that the province of Northern Ireland had been a police state since its foundation in 1920. The partition of Ireland had been contrived to ensure a Protestant/Loyalist majority in the Six Counties. Power was vested in the hands of this distinct cultural grouping, and was maintained by a systematic discrimination against the Catholic minority in every area of public life, most discernibly in housing, jobs, and the exercise of the vote. It was a state of affairs which continued unaltered into the 1970s.

Other instruments of repression included institutionalised gerry-mandering, the use of internment without trial, and other measures under the Special Powers Act allowing detention and interrogation for up to 48 hours – a statutory provision then without parallel in British law. There was also the maintenance of a loyal and, by impli-cation, largely Protestant police force aided and abetted by the B-Specials.

In retrospect it is easy to see how what many regarded as gross abuses of power would result eventually in civil protest and violence. In the months that followed the now famous civil rights march the Stormont government allowed the opportunity of a peaceful solution to the province's troubles to slip away. A swift breakdown of law and order followed. 'Rioting replaced Gaelic football as the most popular activity amongst teenage boys'.[2] The RUC, stretched to its limits and ill-trained to deal with large-scale violence, began to with-draw from nationalist ghettos.

There followed a story which is all too well known: the battle of the Bogside between the RUC and local inhabitants; the introduc-tion of British soldiers on the streets of Ulster; the death of the first British soldier, Robert Curtis, at the hands of the IRA; and Bloody Sunday. There were daily riots; shootings and bombings became commonplace. On August 9, 1971 internment without trial was rein-troduced to Ireland by the Stormont government, but to no avail. Shortly afterwards, Stormont was dissolved by Parliament at West-minster and Direct Rule was introduced. One of the first steps taken by Westminster was to commission Lord Diplock to head an inquiry to 'consider legal measures to deal with terrorist activities in Northern Ireland'.[3]

The Diplock Commission made numerous proposals of signifi-cance, including the recommendation that: 'trial by judge alone should take the place of trial by jury for the duration of the emerg-ency'.[4] This recommendation was incorporated into the Emergency Provisions Act 1973 in these terms: 'A trial on indictment for a sche-duled offence shall be conducted by the court without a jury.' The schedule referred to contained all the most serious criminal offences including murder, robbery, and kidnapping, which arise, though not always, out of terrorist activities.

The suspension of jury trial

The debate

Two arguments were advanced in support of the suspension of jury trials in Northern Ireland: perverse verdicts (usually acquittals in favour of Loyalist defendants), and the danger of jurors being intimidated. It seems that no other reasons were canvassed by the Diplock Commission or in Parliamentary debates. Over the years both factors have achieved the status of self-evident truths, the basis for all political debate.

Much was made of 'dangerously perverse verdicts' in the press and in the Parliamentary debates of the then Emergency Provisions Bill 1973. However, while most of the opponents of the reform conceded that this was indeed a danger if not a reality the actual evidence of perverse verdicts was sketchy. Even the Diplock Commission concluded: 'We have not had our attention drawn to complaints of convictions that were plainly perverse and complaints of acquittals which were perverse are rare.'[5]

Amongst certain members of the judiciary there was concern that the sectarian unrest would give rise to wrongful convictions. Without doubt this was a wholly laudable concern but, without any knowledge of the evidence upon which the concern was based, it is difficult to know what weight should be attached to it. What exactly was the extent of the problem? Were these concerns based on mere anxieties? Were they occasioned by verdicts which were suspect or even plainly wrong? There is simply no evidence on which a considered judgment may be made. Some evidence suggests that perverse acquittals were a problem in relation to Loyalist defendants, but if we are to accept the conclusion of the Diplock Commission this problem was a minor one.

Most commentators attribute the difficulty, such as it was, to two factors. First, at the time the eligibility to sit as a juror in Northern Ireland was subject to a property qualification which a disproportionate section of the Catholic/nationalist community was unable to satisfy. The second reason was an apparent perception in the eyes of many, not least among some members of the judiciary,[6] that violence by Loyalist paramilitaries was in reaction to IRA terrorism and therefore less serious or somehow understandable. The juror eligibility problem was solved the following year when the property qualification was abolished for non-scheduled and civil cases. As to the second difficulty, it is doubtful now whether there are still many individuals who would be prepared to say that violence by Loyalists is somehow less serious or reprehensible than Republican-inspired violence.

With regard to juror intimidation the Diplock Commission observed that 'the threat of intimidation of witnesses ... extends also to jurors, though not to the same extent'.[7] In fact, though the Gardiner Report was later to collate evidence of 482 witnesses intimidated in a two-and-a-half year period, it seems that the evidence of juror intimidation was slight and anecdotal. This did not stop the proponents of non-jury trial playing upon this factor. Greer and White (the authors of the only lengthy non-Government study of the Diplock Courts) points out that: 'Not a single statistic indicating the scale of juror intimidation in Northern Ireland in the 1969–73 period has ever been produced.'[8]

Of course the risk of juror intimidation was real and would be again if jury trial were to be reintroduced. However, the paucity of evidence advanced in support of both the perverse verdict theory and juror intimidation casts a doubt on the good faith of some of the would-be reformers. If there was good evidence that the jury system was coming under 'strain' why were the alternatives to suspension of jury trial not explored at the time?

It seems now that the advocates of a return to jury trial have come to be regarded as either naive, on the extreme fringes of political thought, or worse, as subversive. Yet Greer and White's recent study concluded: 'the evidence which was then presented to justify the introduction of non-jury courts was seriously deficient and at the most indicated that eligibility for jury service should have been democratised, the section of jurors randomised, and the identity of jurors concealed'.

Ulterior motives for suspending jury trial
Many legal political commentators, both then and now,[9] believe that the real reason for suspension of jury trial can be deduced from the Commission's terms of reference, which were to consider 'what arrangements for the administration of justice in Northern Ireland could be made in order to deal more effectively with terrorist organisations by bringing to book, otherwise than by internment by the Executive, individuals involved in terrorist cases'. In other words,

internment was recognised as a short-term measure but an alternative was required, although never publicly canvassed, which would produce a conviction rate acceptable to the Government.[10] Clearly the security forces faced severe difficulties. The normal methods of detection were not open, witnesses were being intimidated, the paramilitaries were becoming more adept at covering their tracks, and more experienced in dealing with interrogation techniques.[11] These factors were acknowledged by Lord Diplock, who stated that evidence would increasingly be forthcoming from one or more of three specific sources: '(1) oral evidence by soldiers or policemen whose protection can more readily be ensured; (2) physical evidence such as fingerprints; and (3) an admissible confession by the accused'.[12]

Faced with these difficulties how could convictions best be obtained? With the benefit of hindsight it is clear that the Diplock Commission would find the single professional judge a preferable tribunal to that of the jury. The consequences must have been obvious: a professional judge will become case-hardened; the conviction rate will increase. This argument is sometimes said to be clichéd, and it may be so, but it is borne out by statistics[13] and by professional judgement of those who practise in the Diplock Courts.

The decision to suspend jury trial may also be seen as an enabling provision. It must have been realised that certain other proposals of the Commission (together with other measures that might in time appear appropriate) to combat terrorism might prove unpalatable to juries, a notable example of this being the proposal to abrogate the Common Law rule requiring all confessions to be voluntary. This proposal was adopted by the Government and enacted in the Emergency Provisions Act 1973, Section 6. Henceforth all confessions were to be admissible unless obtained by torture or inhuman or degrading treatment. In the circumstances it was seen as a necessary if distasteful reform. Few foresaw the consequences.

In a subsequent criminal trial this provision was construed by McGonigal L.J. to mean that during the course of prolonged interrogation it was 'open to an interviewer to use a moderate degree of physical maltreatment for the purpose of inducing a person to make a statement'.[14] This interpretation may not have been anticipated by the Diplock Commission but the example illustrates the dangers of relaxing constitutional safeguards. Thankfully the 'torturer's charter', as it became known, no longer represents the law.

Restoring the status quo

There is a compelling argument that the suspension of a constitutional right ought always to be a measure of the last resort. There is always a danger that the right will not be reinstated for reasons of expediency or just plain complacency. It is important to remember in this context that the suspension of jury trial was intended to be a temporary measure, but 18 years later the so-called 'Diplock Courts' remain the cornerstone of the criminal justice system in Northern Ireland. It is true that the 1975 Gardiner report reiterated the necessity for non-jury criminal courts but it also expressed the view that the jury trial 'should be restored to Northern Ireland as soon as possible'[15]. As yet we seem to be no nearer achieving this pious hope. The latest review of the emergency legislation, carried out by Sir George Baker in 1984, opposed the reintroduction of jury trial. Indeed, the report expressed a considerable degree of antipathy towards the concept of jury trial in any context.[16] The emergency legislation, involving as it did the abrogation of constitutional rights, has gradually become the norm.

Implications for the trial process

1. *Case-hardening*

Lord Diplock observed that: 'an incidental benefit of the decision to suspend jury trial would be to shorten trials so as to enable more cases to be dealt with by the same number of judges'.[17] This ignored, or at least discounted, the possibility that judges might become case-hardened. Perhaps it was not anticipated that the 'emergency' would last for so long.

Put simply the case-hardening argument runs as follows: prior to the trial the judge will have read the depositions of prosecution witnesses and will have become well versed with the nature of the prosecution case. The witnesses tend to be police officers who are trained and usually experienced in giving evidence. Their evidence, observers say, is delivered in a measured business-like manner, often in stark contrast to that of the defendant and any witnesses he might have.

In the majority of trials the only evidence is an alleged confession. It therefore follows that most trials are determined on this issue. Slowly and almost imperceptibly the judge becomes jaded by a succession of cases with nothing much to distinguish one from another. There are few straight knockouts; rather, the same points are scored in each cross-examination; the same arguments advanced. With the best will in the world the judge becomes case-hardened, and with that hardening the burden of proof shifts from the prosecution to the defence. To be a judge in such circumstances requires integrity and intellectual ability of the highest order. Even these qualities may not be enough. It is a plausible scenario, particularly in view of the length of time the Diplock Courts have been in operation. There is some empirical evidence to support this argument. A study conducted by Boyle[18] concluded that: 'it is noticeable that in contested cases ... juries over the period have acquitted on average more frequently than judges' and, more significantly, 'judge trials show a pattern of declining acquittal rates'.

Real acquittal rates are probably even lower when one considers the impact of another disturbing creature of the Diplock system – plea bargaining. In a nutshell this means that defendants are persuaded that the system offers poor prospect of acquittal and agree to a deal offered by the prosecution, taking whatever 'credit' the judge is inclined to give for a plea of guilty. This scenario is borne out to a certain extent by the rate of guilty pleas – 88.5% in 1986[19] – a figure which is much higher than in mainland Britain.

2. Confessions

We have already noted that because of the problems outlined in respect of the collection of evidence, the Common Law test of admissibility of a confession was abolished. By virtue of the Northern Ireland (Emergency Provisions) Act 1978 a confession is admissible against a defendant unless obtained by the use of torture or inhuman or degrading treatment. Under the terms of the section it is incumbent upon the defendant to raise prima-facie evidence that the confession was obtained in breach of the section before the prosecution is called on to rebut it. Thereafter the allegation by the defendant must be refuted beyond reasonable doubt. This in itself represents a significant derogation from the burden of proof under the Common Law.

Statutory powers of detention have given teeth to the provisions relating to the admissibility of confessions. Detention of suspects for three or even seven days has become common and is in sharp contrast to the workaday provisions of the Police and Criminal Evidence Act 1984, which is designed largely to ensure that confessions are obtained fairly.

Unsurprisingly, the RUC has become heavily dependent on confessions to secure convictions. On this point we note that a large sample of cases was examined by the Bennett Committee,[20] which observed that 'in 75-80% of these cases, the prosecution case depended wholly or mainly on the confession of the accused'. The combination of these factors has contributed to ill-treatment of suspects in the custody of the RUC (this claim is supported by a substantial body of evidence).[21] In the light of these findings it is disturbing to note that the conclusion of one study over a four-year period was that 'only 32 alleged confessions have been declared inadmissible ... out of a total number of cases falling not far short of 4,000'.[22]

3. Determination of mode of trial

This is at present determined by reference to Schedule 4 of the Northern Ireland (Emergency Provisions) Act 1978 (as amended). If the offence charged is listed in the schedule the case will be tried by a non-jury court.

The offences in the Schedule are capable of being committed by a person with no paramilitary or political motive. The Attorney-General for Northern Ireland may certify that certain scheduled offences shall be treated as though they were non-scheduled and triable accordingly by judge and jury. It would seem, however, that this discretion has been used sparingly, and as a result defendants with no paramilitary connections find themselves before the Diplock Courts. One commentator estimates that some 40% of defendants fall into this category.[23]

Restoring jury trial?

If success is to be measured by a high conviction rate then the Diplock Courts have been successful. But at what cost? Unfortunately they have had the effect of providing a major propaganda boost to the IRA. The problem is not just a matter of the loss of trial by jury, but also the concomitant changes in the law, such as the reversal of the burden of proof in cases involving possession of firearms and explosives, and the admissibility of confessions. There has also been widespread use of the 'supergrass' as a tactic in the war against terrorism. This has often involved the payment of substantial sums of money to accomplices as well as offering immunity from prosecution in return for their turning Queen's evidence.

These features of the criminal justice system in Northern Ireland have been exploited both there and abroad by the IRA and Sinn

Fein. Their task has been made considerably easier because, taken individually, each of the factors gives genuine cause for concern. Taken together these features represent a massive derogation from what most Western countries recognise as due process.

The opposite side of the argument is put by those who say that normal process will allow terrorists to escape justice. There is some force in this proposition. However, the necessity for emergency legal measures must be measured against other factors, including the denial of fundamental rights and privileges which are enjoyed by citizens throughout the rest of Britain.

The courts no longer enjoy the confidence of much of the public in Northern Ireland. In particular, the sense of disillusionment and cynicism harboured by a large section of the Catholic/nationalist community has been heightened by the operation of the Diplock Courts. It is not easy to offer a remedy for this situation. There is, however, a prerequisite for a return to normality: confidence in the legal system. Without such confidence it is not possible to win over that significant proportion of society whose acquiescence makes terrorism possible.

Most commentators are agreed that the key to the solution lies in involving the community in the system of criminal justice: a return to jury trial being the obvious long-term solution. Other short-term measures have been suggested by a variety of interested parties: a three-judge court (the Irish government), the introduction of lay assessors (Messrs Boyle, Hadden, and Hillyard, and the introduction of a cross-border court to deal with terrorist offences.

There is also a growing body of opinion that some attempt should be made to return to jury trial in the near future. The successful restoration of jury trial is a measure which would make a fundamental contribution to confidence in the rule of law. It is a process whereby ordinary people are allowed and encouraged to participate in their own system of justice, requiring education and the definition and acceptance of individual responsibilities. As things stand in Northern Ireland there are precious few opportunities for individuals from the different sides of the community to meet and perhaps find common values and objectives.

It is encouraging to note that despite the existence of terrorism and large-scale organised crime in other jurisdictions, notably France, Corsica, and Italy, these states have maintained their own variations of trial by jury. In Italy the war against the Mafia is perhaps the best example. Only a few years ago the Italian courts hosted the largest criminal trials in the Western world; over 250 defendants stood trial accused of Mafia-related crimes. The case was tried by a combination of judges and 16 lay assessors. Besides the complement of judges and lay assessors there were a number of 'alternates' ready to stand if any member of the court was murdered. Despite the very considerable difficulties the trial appears to have been conducted with minimum derogation from due process and most of the defendants were convicted.

There would of course be considerable difficulties to be overcome before a successful transition can be brought about in Northern Ireland. It has been suggested that the greatest difficulty would be the danger of interference with jurors by the paramilitaries. If it seems likely that the paramilitaries would attempt to interfere with juries the problem must be met before a return to jury trial can be undertaken. There will also be jurors who may be unable or unwilling to decide cases while disregarding their community loyalties. Although the numbers of such jurors might be small it is worth considering how these problems may be overcome.

Proposals for a reintroduction of jury trial

Protecting jurors

Protection of jurors can best be achieved by ensuring their anonymity. The practicalities of achieving juror anonymity are less daunting than one might at first suppose. A number of legal commentators (notably Jennings and Wolchover,[24] and Greer and White), have set out detailed proposals to this end. The consensus of opinion is that the identity of jurors can be concealed from all (including defence and prosecution lawyers) but a few summoning staff. During the course of a trial jurors would be seated within sight of the witness box but not the dock or the public gallery. They would have access to a hotline in case of intimidation. Variants of these safeguards have been adopted at one time or another in certain English courts to deal with similar problems.

A further suggestion canvassed by Greer and White is the creation of trip-wire offences to deter nobblers. Such offences might be used against those loitering or taking photographs without good reason in the vicinity of a court-house hearing the trial of a scheduled offence.

Finally, there is the possibility of reintroducing the sequestering of jurors if it was proved that there had been an attempt to interfere with the jury.

Summoning and selection

No vetting would take place save for checks by the summoning officer to ensure that the jurors were not ineligible or disqualified. In this respect we have already noted that there are plans to link the police national computer to all Crown Courts, a system which would make this reform practical and inexpensive.

Without prejudice to the principle of juror anonymity, there is scope for a further safeguard: that of a jury *voir dire* and challenge for cause along the lines suggested in Chapter 4. The cumulative effect of these reforms would be to obviate the need for vetting by the police or security services.

Finally, Greer and White have suggested that applications for excusals by those living in hardline Republican or Loyalist areas ought to receive especially sympathetic consideration.

Verdicts

Inevitably there would be a small percentage of jurors who would be unable or unwilling to set aside their loyalties and try cases solely on the evidence. It seems likely that some of these would be sifted out by reason of criminal convictions or on the *voir dire*. We accept that there remains a risk of perversity in the occasional juror and therefore that an argument exists in favour of the use of majority verdicts. It is perhaps the only instance in which majority verdicts can be justified without recourse to considerations of cost and efficiency.

Phasing in jury trial

This would probably be best done gradually, the results being monitored before a complete return to jury trial is effected. We have already noted that a substantial number of defendants tried by the Diplock Courts have no connections with paramilitary organisations. For this reason at least one commentator has suggested that this category of defendant ought to be tried by a judge and jury in any event. This might well be a useful starting-point to bring about a return to trial by jury.

A second stage might encompass a concept that Greer and White have labelled 'contingent jury trial'. This idea has been canvassed in a number of forms; in essence it means that every trial should commence before judge and jury. If it were proved that there had been an attempt to interfere with a juror the trial would be halted and heard by a different judge and jury. Any further attempt to interfere with a juror and the case would then be heard by a judge sitting alone.

Chapter 9

Jury Trial: Arguments For and Against, and the Alternatives

It is a truly remarkable fact that jury trial has been the usual method of dealing with serious criminal cases since the thirteenth century. Its main attraction has been its role as a broadly independent tribunal. But it has also come to fulfil certain ancillary functions; a socio-political role and a constitutional role.

Perhaps the most remarkable feature of jury trial is that although every juror is required to swear or affirm to give 'a true verdict according to the evidence', this has never been what society has wanted or expected from juries. If this were all that were required, then the professional tribunal, a judge or judges, magistrates both lay and professional would all provide a cheaper, better fact-finding body and, for the authorities, a more reliable forum. And as we have shown, this seems to be a trend being sought and obtained at an increasingly fast rate. It is a process which reflects, for a number of reasons, a lack of confidence in juries.

From what does this crisis of confidence arise? In part it stems from a belief that trial by jury is an anachronism; that it attempts to fulfil a role that is no longer appropriate. The law is flexible and, the argument runs, mercy is the prerogative of the judge.

After all, say the detractors of jury trial, our system of criminal justice has improved beyond recognition. Defendants are entitled as of right to be represented – it was not always so. Legal aid is now available on a wide scale. The majority of our judiciary are fair, manifestly so, and we have a structured appeals procedure. Penalties under the law have been drastically mitigated, oppressive prosecutions are unusual and, almost as important, the appearance of oppression.

has diminished.

Given these by no means modest improvements, the necessity for jury trial is arguably less clear-cut. The jury can be presented as an irrational institution at odds with a society which prides itself on a rational approach to its problems. Looked at objectively, we take individuals, many of whom do not wish to be co-opted and who have no training in the law. We inundate them with complex legal argument, saturate them with evidence, and send them away to deliberate in secret and return a verdict for which they give no reasons. Viewed in this light we have an extraordinary if not anachronistic system. But are we so confident of our modern institutions that we can allow the jury system to be dismantled piecemeal?

Recent years have witnessed the gradual erosion of the right to trial by jury. Unfortunately the debate has tended to revolve round single issues: majority verdicts; vetting; challenging; the withdrawal of the right to trial for so-called minor offences; and the suspension of jury trial in Northern Ireland. Each reform has been debated and implemented piecemeal. Each, of course, is justified on the grounds of expense, delay, necessity, or some other seemingly compelling reason, but the cumulative effect has been to undermine seriously the concept of jury trial in this country. In its determination to reform, rationalise, and curb costs society has been in danger of losing sight of the major arguments of principle as they apply to the present day. And it is to these that we now turn.

Arguments for the retention of jury trial

Justice in individual cases

Lord Devlin wrote 'the law may be made as flexible as possible but the Justice of the case cannot go beyond the furthest point to which the law can be stretched. Trial by jury is a unique institution ... to enable juries to go beyond that point.'[1] It has long been recognised that verdicts of juries may be founded on factors which have little to do with the evidence. We have outlined earlier some of the categories of cases in which such verdicts were once common: dislike of a particular law; distaste for the sentence which would follow conviction; or in reaction to arbitrary or oppressive conduct by the State.

Such verdicts, once run-of-the-mill, are no longer common, largely because our system of justice is inestimably more just and humane than it was even at the turn of the century. Unfortunately this has led many to argue mistakenly that because our system of criminal law has attained a degree of justice and humanity, we can therefore dispense with the jury. Such an argument gives insufficient weight to the role of the jury in first bringing about and then maintaining this state of affairs.

As every practitioner will testify equitable jury verdicts still occur, and though direct conflict between judge and jury is rare, it still crops up in a handful of cases every year. We referred in Chapter 2 to the most recent and well publicised case of Jennings where the jury refused to abide by a direction to convict. These interventions have merit, if only because they force lawyers to re-examine and justify crucial decisions in the trial process: the decisions to prosecute, to convict, and to punish. It keeps the law and lawyers in touch with society. This brings us to the second advantage of the jury trial: accountability.

Accountability

In essence this means that the State has to justify every serious prosecution of an individual to twelve of his peers chosen at random from the community. It is one of the checks which keeps the State in tune with society at large. It introduces a healthy democratic element into the administration of justice. Significantly, Knittel and Seiler record that:

a number of continental countries abolished trial by jury after they had abandoned democratic principles. This was the case with Italy in 1931 after the Fascist Party had formed the Government. In Portugal trial by jury was abolished in 1927 after Gomez de Costa had established a dictatorship. In Spain trial by jury was given up when General Franco seized power in 1936, and in France the Vichy Government of 1941 was responsible for the abolition of the jury.[2]

France has since restored the jury and after the death of Franco in 1975 the new Spanish constitution made provision for a return to jury trial. This reform has yet to come to pass, perhaps because jury trial is an expensive and awkward institution which offers no advantage to the Executive. Even so, the link between jury trial and democracy is a strong one; it certainly confers an element of legitimacy on prosecutions brought by the State.

Under the jury system the prosecution must explain to the jury in plain and simple English what it alleges the defendant has done. The language is therefore one which the defendant will understand.

It is an aspect of the maxim that justice must be seen to be done, and it is particularly important in complex cases. In carrying out this function the prosecution fulfils a subsidiary role in educating citizens as to their rights and duties under the law. On the other hand this process allows jurors to contribute by defining the limits of criminality by acting as a check on the power of the State or simply by interpreting concepts such as dishonesty, self-defence and the freedoms of expression and assembly.

The issues are particularly clear-cut in relation to the dividing line between obscenity and art. For who should be the moral guardians of society? The Government? Or its appointed nominee – the Arts Council perhaps, or Mary Whitehouse?

It is worth noting that the Republic of Eire operates a censorship board whose decisions have been a source of controversy for many years. Norman St John Stevas observed that as late as the 1960s the list of banned books included Graham Greene's *Heart of the Matter* and *The End of the Affair* as well as books by Koestler, Gide, Proust, Maugham, Huxley, Faulkner, Lawrence and Forster, along with 'nearly every Irish writer of distinction'.

In England the stipendiary magistracy fulfilled an analogous role in the exercise of their powers under the Obscene Publications Act of 1857. In 1915 it was a magistrate who ordered 1000 copies of *The Rainbow* to be destroyed. *Ulysses* went the same way in 1923, and much more recently so did *Fanny Hill* and *Last Exit to Brooklyn*.

We have already noted that recent prosecutions before juries have met with rather less success. An insight into the thinking of the anti-jury lobby can be gained by looking at the recent prosecution of Michael Bogdanov, Director of *The Romans in Britain*. The play contains a controversial scene in which a Roman soldier buggers a native Celt. Mary Whitehouse immediately brought a private prosecution against Bogdanov for 'procuring an act of gross indecency.' At the close of the prosecution case and after the trial judge pronounced himself satisfied that there was a case to answer in law, the prosecution was withdrawn. It was a clever tactic designed to make a neat legal point but in order to be sure of success it was necessary to avoid that last awkward hurdle; the verdict of the jury.

A safeguard against abuse of power by the judges

The jury has long been a safeguard (albeit an imperfect one) against what Blackstone termed 'the violence and partiality of judges appointed by the Crown'.[3] Judicial bias has always been a feature of criminal trials throughout our history. It appears sometimes in the form of outright hostility towards the defendant, but is more usually reflected in a subtle bias which pervades the whole trial. Examples of the former are well documented. Notable examples include the trials of Throckmorton, Raleigh, Lilburne, Penn and Mead, and William Hone. The latter category boasts Judge Jeffreys of the Bloody Assizes and in particular his prolonged browbeating of the jury which ultimately secured the conviction of Dame Alice Lisle for treason.* Another example is that of Judge Braxfield's conduct of the Scottish Treason Trials of the 1790s. One of his comments to a juror is worth recalling: 'Come awae Master Horner, Come awae and help us hang anae of these damn scoundrels.'[4]

These might seem rather dated examples but in fact, although most of our judges are eminently fair, judicial bias remains a feature of criminal trials in this country. Cases still abound in which there is open hostility towards counsel for the defence, the aside to the jury and the biased summing up.

It is the summing up which gives most scope for abuse. Very often the form of words appear to convey, at least on paper, impartiality but are in reality a veiled direction to convict. History provides us with many famous examples of judicial bias in criminal trials. Notable examples include the summing up by Fitzjames Stephens J in the trial of Florence Maybrick for the murder of her husband in 1889. There was also the trial of Derek Bentley and Christopher Craig in 1952 for the murder of a police officer. The summing up by the trial judge, Lord Goddard, was heavily criticised on the grounds of bias against the accused. The Court of Appeal declined to interfere and Derek Bentley, aged nineteen, was hanged. His co-defendant Christopher Craig escaped the death penalty because he was a juvenile. Two more recent examples of judicial bias include the summing up in the trial of Doctor Stephen Ward and, more lately, the case of Clive Ponting. And these are not isolated instances. It has been pointed out by Keith Evans that the most common ground of appeal is that the judge summed up unfairly against the accused.

The Court of Appeal provides a remedy for the grosser examples of judicial bias. We have already noted in Chapter 2 that a number of convictions were recently overturned on this ground. In the case

---

* Dame Alice Lisle was sentenced to be hung, drawn and quartered. As an act of clemency this sentence was set aside in favour of simple beheading.

of *Berrada* the Court of Appeal felt it necessary to state that the duty of a trial judge was to sum up with 'clarity and impartiality and without exaggeration or sarcasm'.

Judicial bias may also arise unconsciously or through a lapse of judgement (though it is no more acceptable for that). An example of such a lapse arose in the case of *R. v. Renshaw* (*The Times*, 1 August 1988). In this case a young woman was sentenced for contempt of court after she had refused to give evidence against her former boyfriend whom she alleged had attacked her. The Court of Appeal criticised the judge (who enjoys a well-deserved reputation for integrity) on the grounds that he attempted to conduct the prosecution himself and failed to allow counsel for the defence to argue his case.

There are, however, more significant problems in this area of the law. One Queen's Counsel recently wrote of the judiciary: 'There are many who have not even learned what I would have thought was the first lesson in the art of being a judge, how to convey the impression of being fair.'[5] D.N.Pritt wrote '. . . the bias is quite deliberate, as when judges try to steer the jury by a mixture of comment and innuendo'.[6] The phenomenon is widely recognised amongst practitioners and has been discussed elsewhere.[7] Keith Evans recently suggested a radical solution: that we adopt the American practice where (in general) the judge may sum up as to the law but may not address the jury on the facts. The proposal enjoys a surprising degree of support amongst members of the Criminal Bar. At present, however, the problem continues to provide considerable difficulties for lawyers appearing for the defence. In such cases it is the jury which is the last line of defence and often jurors are sufficiently sophisticated to understand what is happening.

Political prosecutions
The value of the jury as an agent for resisting the power of the State in political prosecutions has been seriously questioned in recent years.[8] These reservations deserve to be given weight but we have recited some of the evidence to the contrary in Chapters 1 and 2.

We would argue that the failure of juries to protect individuals has often been a result of another malfunction in the legal process, such as a biased judge, or a State-inspired prosecution, or some other less obvious interference with the jury. At this stage we need do no more than point out that the jury has often been the sole, if imperfect, protection for individuals against the power of the State. Of course we would accept that even in this respect it has often been found wanting. The case of the Tolpuddle Martyrs is perhaps an example of a jury acting for narrow class interests or at least failing to stand against a biased judge who effectively conducted the prosecution himself.[9]

The efficacy of the jury as a barrier against the power of the State can, however, be measured by the steps taken by governments and the judiciary to undermine and muzzle juries. The methods have varied: bullying and threatening (Dean of St Asaph, 1783); fining and imprisoning (Penn and Mead, 1670); employing special juries; and packing, vetting and checking jurors.

Much of this, with the exception of vetting, will be thought to lie in the past. This is not quite correct. What, after all, is the purpose of raising the age limit of jurors to 70 if this is not a form of packing?[10] It may be called enlarging the pool or even redressing the age balance, but that is a rose by another name.

On the other hand, Professor Cornish has rightly pointed out that: 'for more than a century juries have played a very minor role in the prosecution of political offenders. In the delicate area of the right to express public opinions, the activities of salvationists, suffragettes, Irish Home Rulers, Fascists, Communists and others have kept the courts busy when disturbances have been created but nearly always it has been the magistrates who have heard the cases.'[11] The reason for this is clear. The offences, often quite serious, for which this motley group of people have appeared before the courts have not often carried the right of jury trial. Although this was a period in which juries did little to enhance the reputation of the jury system as a protection for individual liberties, the prosecution clearly preferred to have such cases tried by magistrates.

We have already pointed out that manipulating the trial venue is nothing new, and this continues to be a tactic employed by prosecutors. Anecdotal evidence suggests that the practice of manipulating the trial venue has become particularly prevalent in the last few years. The practice is most objectionable when used in dealing with public order offences arising out of political or industrial disputes. The trials arising out of the disturbances at Southall (1979) and the National Graphical Association dispute with Eddie Shah's firm at Warrington and the Miners' strike of 1984 are recent examples of this tactic. The prosecutors have been shrewd in their choice of forum. Magistrates have always proved to be a more receptive alternative to juries in this respect.

Arguments against the retention of jury trial

Expense and delay

The twin problems of expense and delay are inextricably bound together in the trial process. In recent years they have proved to be considerable and legitimate causes of concern for both the Lord Chancellor and the Home Office.

Jury trial is an expensive mode of trial particularly in the sphere of fraud trials where, for example, 'the photocopying bill alone can run into thousands of pounds'.[12] It cannot be denied that it is also a lengthy mode of trial compared with trial by a single judge or stipendiary magistrate, even with trial by a lay bench. Again, fraud trials are a particular example of how a case may be lengthened by the presence of a jury. This, however, may not necessarily be the fault of the jury. Moreover, if the bulk of the Roskill recommendations relating to pre-trial procedures (some of which have already appeared in the Criminal Justice Acts 1987/8) are adopted and rigorously applied, much of the time now lost in jury trials would be saved.

The problems of expense and delay are not new. As long ago as 1973 the James Committee noted that: 'The machinery of the superior courts is not only turning too slowly; even at its present rate of rotation it is creaking under the strain.'[13] The situation has not improved; quite the reverse. Since the implementation of the James Committee proposals, the number of cases committed for trial at the Crown Court annually has risen from 50,800 to 98,000.[14] Appeals against conviction have also risen sharply by nearly a quarter. The Home Office has unsuccessfully attempted to keep pace with the increased case-load by undertaking a number of measures, including the provision of extra court space, improved efficiency, and the appointment of a considerable number of new judges.

Inevitably, the result of the increase in work has been increased cost to the taxpayer and a delay in the trial process. There is much truth in the saying 'justice delayed is justice denied'; witnesses move, memories fade, and the effect of a deterrent sentence is muted when the offence has become stale. Of all defendants remanded in custody nearly half will be acquitted, and of the total number no less than 15% will serve 13 weeks (many much longer) before their trial is called. Furthermore, the conditions in which they are held have deteriorated sharply in recent years.

Largely for these reasons the Home Office has continued to press for the alleviation of the Crown Court case-load by transferring cases to the jurisdiction of the magistrates. The Justices' Clerks Society has also figured prominently in arguing for a redistribution of criminal business in this way. The Society has relied principally on the argument that magistrates' courts provide a suitable alternative to jury trial for all but the most serious of cases. The Society has also argued forcefully that magistrates' courts are easily 'the most cost-effective system of justice in the country'.[15] The arguments put forward are (a) the caseload: magistrates deal with 97% of all criminal business and also dispose of a considerable civil case-load; (b) administration costs: in the magistrates' courts income from fines and fees outweigh the costs of the service to society; (c) legal aid costs: providing legal aid to defendants in the Crown Courts costs approximately four times the equivalent expense in the magistrates' court.

Too many acquittals

The great debate

It has long been recognised that juries acquit more readily than do magistrates, but there has been concern in recent years that juries acquit far too regularly. This topic first became a matter of public concern when in 1966 the *New Law Journal* published the results of a survey carried out at the behest of the Association of Chief Police Officers. The survey purported to show that the true acquittal rate in jury trials was 39%.[16] At first sight this is a startlingly high figure and it reinforced a fairly widespread belief that professional criminals were 'getting off'.

It was a point of view expounded by Sir Robert Mark in his now famous Dimbleby lecture of 1973. He directly criticised juries for their refusal to convict and for acquittals which were 'blatantly perverse'.[17] In 1974 he instigated the *Metropolitan Police Study of Acquittal Rates* (published that year). The study purported to show that 40% of all defendants at the Crown Court were acquitted. This apparently confirmed the *New Law Journal* figures of nearly a decade earlier. Recent Home Office research has confirmed what every practitioner in the criminal courts knows to be true, that 'the chances of acquittal are significantly higher in the Crown Court than in magistrates' courts'.[18]

The issue has continued to simmer over the intervening years. The Anarchist trial in 1979 and the Ponting trial are but two examples of instances when critics of the system argued that the jury simply did not act in accordance with the evidence.

The figures

The evidence shows that the great majority of defendants committed for trial plead guilty. The *Association of Chief Police Officers Survey* estimated the figure to be 64%. The *Metropolitan Police Survey* suggested 80%; Zander in 1974 suggested 70%; Baldwin and McConville's survey made the total 79.2%.

Acquittal rates calculated as a percentage of those who pleaded not guilty to all charges were as follows:

Association of Chief Police Officers	39%
Metropolitan Police Survey	40%
Zander	average 42.5%

A major criticism of the early studies by the Metropolitan Police and the Association of Chief Police Officers is that they do not differentiate between acquittals directed by the judge (because of the weakness of the prosecution case) and acquittals returned by juries. A further criticism is that the figures do not take into account prosecutions brought for policy reasons, often without any real hope or expectation of success. Both these criticisms are well illustrated in a study by McCabe and Purves.[19] This study involved the analysis of 173 jury trials which ended in acquittals. The authors of the study assessed the verdicts of acquittal by interviewing the judges, lawyers, and police officers involved in each trial. A breakdown of the 173 acquittals is as follows:

Directed by the trial judge	58
Policy prosecutions	44
Failure of prosecution witnesses	8
Weak cases	20
Defendant's explanation decisive	28
Acquittal termed wayward	15
Total	*173*

It should be noted that no less than one-third of all acquittals were directed by the judge because the prosecution case was too weak to go to the jury. Other research of the same period[20] confirms this very high rate of directed acquittals, while later research puts the figure even higher.[21]

McCabe and Purves observe a startling number of acquittals resulting from policy prosecutions which were brought not because there was cogent evidence of the commission of a crime but in the words of the authors 'for reasons of general policy or the need to satisfy particular types of complainants'. It may be that when the Crown Prosecution Service beds down, this sort of prosecution will be eliminated.

The 64 acquittals which come under the heading of 'policy prosecutions' and 'other weak cases' indicate that on an objective assessment of the evidence acquittals were expected in 122 of the 173 cases.

Both McCabe and Purves and Zander found a similarly small proportion of 'perverse' verdicts. It is, however, difficult to assess whether these verdicts were actually perverse since the views of the jurors involved were not canvassed. All that can safely be said is that the professionals, all of whom had an interest in the result, disagreed with the jury. If juries were to act merely in accordance with the views of lawyers and policemen they could be dispensed with easily.

None the less the figure is sufficiently great to require some explanation. Baldwin and McConville's study in Birmingham suggested that the juries were returning verdicts which were generally deemed reasonable by judges, lawyers, and police, although they themselves have expressed personal reservations that 'the jury appeared on occasion to be over-ready to acquit those who were probably guilty and insufficiently prepared to protect the possibly innocent'. The authors stated that their confidence in the jury system was 'shaken'.[22]

Shadow juries

The shadow jury work carried out by McCabe and Purves is of some assistance, though one must be wary of attaching too much weight to such research for the obvious reason that one cannot be sure that a shadow jury will act in the same way as a trial jury. With this in mind the conclusions of McCabe and Purves were that there was 'little evidence of perversity' and that 'the shadow jurors showed considerable determination in looking for evidence upon which convictions could be based and when it seemed inadequate were not prepared to follow their hunch'.

Professional criminals

What is to be made of Sir Robert Mark's complaint that professional criminals were evading conviction and that some were 'notching up an astonishing number of acquittals'? The evidence of the academics would seem to be to the contrary (although most of the research is now dated and in need of revision).

Zander's study found no evidence to support the view that a disproportionate number of professional criminals were being acquitted by juries. He rightly hesitated to equate the possession of a criminal record with the term 'professional criminal' but considered it to be a useful indicator. He also noted that 'the worse the record the lower the acquittal rate'. This was a finding supported by McCabe and Purves' shadow jury work and by other research, whose conclusion was that as a group 'professional criminals' were convicted more frequently than any other group of defendants. To an extent this research has been corroborated by an anonymous study – thought to be that of a judge reviewing his case-load – of 257 cases, a study significantly entitled *The Guilty are Convicted*.[23]

Conclusion

We take as our measure of the acquittal rate that suggested by Michael Zander: by expressing the number of not guilty verdicts as a percentage of the defendants pleading not guilty to all counts and deducting from this the number of acquittals directed by judges. Thus the Home Office figures for 1981 give a total acquittal rate of 48%, which subtracting directed acquittals produces a figure of 27%: in fact, barely over the rate of acquittals by magistrates. If the figure is readjusted to take policy prosecutions into account it would decline still further.

It is difficult, if not impossible, to draw from these and other figures conclusions as to the efficacy of the jury system. We would say that the percentage of acquittals is essentially unimportant. What is of importance is how juries reach their verdicts. Since we are denied access to jurors or their deliberations we have to fall back on the informed judgement of professionals and the use of shadow juries. At best it is unsatisfactory; at worst, speculative.

What can be said is that most defendants plead guilty and that those cases which are committed for trial and come before juries are, for the most part, serious cases in which, even if there is no real doubt as to the guilt of the accused, at least the case is hotly and usually ably defended. It can also be said that a reason for the number of acquittals is the delay in bringing cases to court which may affect the 'availability and credibility of prosecution witnesses'.[24] This is clearly a fault of the system and not the jury in these cases.

An institution unfitted to do justice?

Comprehension

What Lord Roskill termed 'the limits of comprehension' has been bluntly, perhaps even a little cruelly, described in these terms: 'Persons whose ordinary occupations are of a humble character rarely qualify as first rate intellectual machines. They are not accustomed to giving sustained attention to the spoken word, and many will have a narrow vocabulary and range of idea.'[25] The problems do not end there; after a recent trial and conviction of two defendants one juror was found to have been deaf and to have missed half the evidence. The Court of Appeal refused to intervene.[26]

After the trial of Penguin Books for publishing *Lady Chatterley's Lover* C.H.Rolph noted that although the defence was one of 'literary merit' no fewer than five of the jury read the oath 'with some difficulty or hesitancy'. Another comment on jury literacy from a slightly later period indicated that 'on no single jury were there fewer than two people who could not read or write'.

In general the only test of literacy is the ability of a juror to read the oath. This may not seem to be a particularly difficult test if he has heard a number of others read it before him. Some quite obviously have difficulties. Some stumble through, some own up straight away that they cannot read well, but it is our experience that others manage to disguise their difficulty. In one, perhaps extreme, example, a trial at the Old Bailey was halted when it was discovered that one of the jurors could speak only a few words of English.

Qualifications and competence

Coexistent with this criticism is the question of qualifications to sit as jurors. The right to sit as a juror is broadly coextensive with the right to vote, subject to an upper age limit of 70. There are no qualifications of literacy or any academic attainments. Persons such as solicitors, who might be thought to be competent to act as jurors, are ineligible. It must be the only institution where knowledge or competence are a positive bar to service.

There is a fair body of anecdotal evidence on how the jury functions. A collection of jurors' experiences are recorded in Barber and Gordon. They include those of Harry Cohen, sitting on a jury which had just retired after a three week case: 'As soon as the court attendant departed the man standing with his back to the door announced in a loud and impassioned voice that no matter what anyone said or if he stayed there for three weeks he would never vote guilty in this case. This announcement was greeted by a stunned silence.' He continues: 'I emerged, quite horrified, and fearful of at any time being placed at the risk of myself being tried by a jury.'

Elwyn Morris recounts that the jury had just retired and were beginning to address their minds to the question when 'the ladies had not moved from their corner, and since I knew one of them I asked her if she and the other two would take their seats at the table. "Oh, you men settle it amongst yourselves", she replied. And the women took no part.'

If only it were merely a case of some jurors failing to take part in the debate. Sadly, it is well established that miscarriages of justice regularly occur. In the United States Judge Jerome Frank collected a number of such cases together in a book (*Not Guilty*). Nor are we immune in England, where there is a substantial public unease over the correctness of convictions in a number of cases. Bob Woffingdon's contribution to the debate – *Miscarriages of Justice* – is the most recent of a number of works on the subject. A cautionary word must be spoken however. Unjust convictions need not be the fault of the jury but some other malfunction in the investigation process or the trial itself. None the less one professor, describing his own experiences as a juror, wrote acidly: 'If the jury is to remain part of the English legal system, it is as well that its proceedings should remain secret.'[27]

Jury-room secrets

Secrecy has been the keystone to jury deliberations. The view of the courts was stated in the Armstrong murder case:

> Reference has been made in the course of the argument to the fact that, after the verdict, there appeared in some newspapers an account of what the writer said was said to him about the evidence with a complete lack of reserve by the juror ... In the opinion of this court nothing could be more improper, deplorable, and dangerous. It may be that some jurymen are not aware that the inestimable value of their verdict is created only by their unanimity, and does not depend upon the process by which they believe they arrived at it.[28]

A year later an application was made for a retrial on the basis that the words attributed to the juryman were not what had been decided in the jury-room. The court dealt swiftly with, and adversely to, that argument.[29]

Matters on the subject of jury secrecy came to a head in the late 1970s. Shortly prior to that the Tenth Criminal Law Revision Committee dealing with the secrets of the jury-room came to the conclusion that they 'did not deem it necessary or desirable to make any statutory provisions to protect the secrecy of the jury-room'. However, when a juror, without reward, wrote in *The New Statesman* about the trial of the Liberal leader Jeremy Thorpe ('Thorpe's trial: How the jury saw it'), the Attorney-General brought contempt proceedings. The court, deciding that proceedings should not issue against the editor, commented that there had been recently a number of articles on discussion in the jury-room. 'In these cases jury-room secrets were revealed in the main for the laudable purpose of informing would-be jurors what to expect when summoned for jury service.'[30]

It was not long, however, before Parliament acted. The Contempt of Court Act 1981 Section 8 (1) states: 'It is a contempt of court to obtain, disclose, or solicit any particulars of statements made, opinions expressed, arguments advanced, or votes cast by members of a jury in the course of their deliberations.' The effect of the section was to shut down all research into the jury and its deliberations.

It is as though it does not matter if the jury gets it right, but when it gets it wrong then it must not be revealed that the error occurred. It is to this that Baldwin and McConville refer when they expressed grave disquiet about the number of convictions which appeared doubtful and the inability of our appeals system to offer effective redress. (A similar criticism was once made of the American trial system by Judge Jerome Frank.)

The point has been illustrated recently in the case of *R. v. Chionye*.[31] After returning a verdict of guilty the jury learned of facts not disclosed to them in the trial and told the judge they had been influenced against the defendant because of this lack of disclosure. The judge questioned the jury foreman in chambers in the presence of counsel with the proceedings being tape-recorded. The Court of Appeal thought this might amount to a breach of Section 8 (1) of the Contempt of Court Act and declined to hear what the jury foreman had said.

A failure to protect minorities
Probably one of the more cogent arguments against the jury and one which surfaces and resurfaces throughout our history is that juries can be swept along on a tide of public hysteria or prejudice and

will convict without due regard to the evidence. One instance is the affair of Titus Oates and the so-called Popish Plot, a classic example of convictions of some two dozen individuals based on religious prejudice and on palpably false evidence.

More recently there are the trials of John William Gott for blasphemous libel. Gott was one of those stalwart, slightly eccentric figures that crop up so regularly in the history books. His obsession was with the atheist ideal. He was convicted four times under the blasphemy laws for advocating atheist ideas in public. His last conviction in 1922 arose out of his selling two pro-atheist pamphlets in the street. *The Rib Tickler* and *Gott and God*, although fairly innocuous atheist tracts, caused a lady passer-by to call out 'disgusting'. In this instance trial by jury was no protection. Despite his ill-health Gott received a sentence of nine months' hard labour and died shortly after leaving prison.

Another no less dramatic example is the so-called Monkey Trial which took place in Daton, Tennessee in 1925. The defendant, John Scopes, a school teacher, was prosecuted for teaching his class Darwin's theory of creation. The prosecution was launched under a state law which prohibited the dissemination of any concepts denying the theory of divine creation. The jury convicted: another example of a jury upholding the narrowest prejudices of society.

Yet more twentieth-century examples of juries ruled by bigotry and hatred can be seen in many trials of negroes in the American south. Perhaps the worst and certainly one of the best-known cases is that of the nine Scottsboro Boys who were alleged to have raped two white girls. In 1931 the Scottsboro Boys were riding boxcar to Memphis. They became involved in a fight with some white youths and threw the latter off the train. The police were alerted and told to 'round up every negro on the train and bring them to Scottsboro'. It was the boys' misfortune that when they were apprehended there were two white girls, Victoria Price, aged 19, and Ruby Bates, two years younger, also in the car. The girls faced the fairly straight choice of a vagrancy charge – with the penalty of a spell in prison – or crying rape. They took the latter course.

The trial took place twelve days later at Scottsboro. Although medical evidence showed that both girls had had sexual intercourse it was not recent. Nevertheless the boys were convicted. The prosecution's invitation to the jury 'Guilty or not, let's get rid of these niggers', went unchecked by the trial judge. Eight were sentenced to death and the ninth, a mere 13 years old, was sentenced to life imprisonment. Seven of the jurors had voted for the death penalty in his case as well. The next year the convictions were overturned on the grounds the defendants had had no adequate counsel.

There was, it seems, no justice to be had from a southern jury. The atmosphere of bigotry was all-pervading. The great New York lawyer, Samuel Leibowitz, brought south for the first retrial, – was charitably described, in some sections of the Alabama state administration, as a 'nigger-loving Jew.'

A number of trials and retrials followed, each successfully appealed. The boys, represented by the International Labor Defense, gradually became pawns in a political battle for the future of the American trial system. One landmark appeal confirmed the principle of the right to adequate counsel. Another appeal was upheld because of the systematic exclusion of blacks from juries throughout Alabama. Eventually, charges against four were dropped, four were parolled and the ninth, Haywood Patterson, the alleged ringleader, escaped after serving seventeen years in prison.

Much more recently in Sweden there was the case of Christer Petterson. This defendant, described in the press as a long-time drug abuser and petty criminal, was tried in the summer of 1989 for the murder of the popular Swedish prime minister, Olaf Palme. The prosecution case seemed weak, resting on 'fleeting glimpse' identification evidence. No motive was ever established, nor was there any forensic evidence linking the defendant to the crime. Petterson was convicted. Interestingly, the conviction was by a six-two majority. The six jurors voted for conviction and the two professional judges favoured acquittal. The conviction was later overturned by the appeal court but not before Petterson had spent many months in prison.

A far more serious miscarriage of justice occurred in the cases of four young Irish people: Paul Hill, Carole Richardson, Patrick Armstrong and Gerard Conlon. These four were found guilty of carrying out the Guildford pub bombings in 1973. A number of people died in the bomb blasts, and the police investigation took place against a background of public outrage. The convictions of the four were based solely on their own confessions. Each of the defendants retracted their confessions, which they alleged had been fabricated or obtained by duress.

The convictions, which became a source of public unease, were the subject of an unsuccessful appeal in 1977. On that occasion, fresh evidence was given by convicted terrorists (the Balcombe Street Gang) who claimed responsibility for the Guildford bombings. The fresh evidence was dismissed by the Court of Appeal as a 'cunning' attempt to deceive the Court.

It was not until the autumn of 1989 after the defendants had spent the best part of fifteen years behind bars that the convictions were overturned in dramatic circumstances. Prosecuting counsel announced that evidence had come to light which indicated that some police officers had perjured themselves at the trial. A contributory factor related to alibi evidence which had been suppressed by the prosecution. Perhaps in these circumstances little blame can be attached to the trial jury. Perhaps also the received wisdom that lay tribunals are particularly prone to prejudice against defendants drawn from unpopular ethnic groupings is too simplistic.

Alternatives to jury trial

What then are the alternatives to the jury system as it is organised in this country? They might conveniently be divided into non-jury alternatives, and other variants on the jury system in Europe, the Commonwealth, and America.

Comparisons, said Dogberry, are 'odorous'. Certainly there are real difficulties in comparing the merits of different jury systems. It is difficult to argue the respective merits of a jury of twelve which may convict on a unanimous vote (as is the case in most states in America), a jury which admits a verdict of guilty by a majority of 10–2 (as in England), and a system which requires only a simple majority. (In Scotland, for example, there is a jury of 15 which may decide guilt on a bare majority but which has an additional alternative – that of not proven – and more exacting rules of evidence.)

Discussion is also hampered unless one has an intimate knowledge of the practical workings of the different systems. It is, for example, difficult to accept the proposition of Blumberg, a New York lawyer, that 'whatever the system's merits or drawbacks may be, the fact is that defendants shun a jury trial'.[32] That is not the case in England and Wales and it can be understood only if the reader has a proper knowledge of the American system of 'plea' or more properly 'sentence' bargaining, something outlawed in English courts.

Blumberg offers this further interesting comment, which would seem at odds with the experience of most criminal practitioners in this country: 'an even more critical factor for the individual accused is his knowledge (whether he senses it intuitively or has learned it from his jail companions or his lawyer) that juries are notoriously prone to convict'. This may have been the situation obtaining in New York 20 years ago but it is not the situation in England in the late 1980's. This may be a function of many factors: for instance, in France the jury always hears of the previous convictions of the accused during the trial, and in certain states of America the defendant may be cross-examined about his criminal record. In England, however, the rule is that no mention of the defendant's bad character may be made unless he wrongly asserts his good character or attacks the character of prosecution witnesses, in which case he may be cross-examined about his past (if indeed he chooses to give evidence). These are just some of the crucial differences in trial systems which are broadly similar and illustrate the dangers of drawing comparisons too readily. With these reservations in mind, there now follow some details of the workings of other jury systems.

America

Jury trial is still the most usual method of trying serious criminal cases. The Supreme Court established in 1966 the right to trial by an impartial jury. In 1969, on an appeal from a decision by the Supreme Court of Louisiana, the Supreme Court laid down the right of defendants to be tried by a jury in criminal cases above the petty level. In federal cases there is a requirement that verdicts be unanimous. Although most states require a unanimous verdict, in Louisiana, for example, there may be a 9–3 majority, whilst in Oregon a 10–2 or 11–1 verdict will suffice.

In 1978 the Supreme Court reviewed the growing practice of mini-juries in non-petty criminal cases. Georgia had been using a five-member panel and the Supreme Court ruled this could not stand. Again in Louisiana there had been 5–1 majority verdicts and these too were ruled unconstitutional. It can be seen readily that a mini-jury is likely to be far less representative of the community than the standard jury of twelve.

There has, however, been an increasing trend in some states, to offer the defendants the option of waiving jury trial in favour of trial by a single judge. Similar provisions exist in other jurisdictions, notably Australia, Canada, and New Zealand.

As in France, most American states allow the jury to take part in the sentencing process. In a few states the verdict and sentence are both the preserve of juries. In all states the trial judge may sum up the law but not the facts. In California, for example, it is usual for the judge to invite the attorneys to ask him what directions (e.g. as to the burden of proof, corroboration, etc) they wish him to give. It is usual for the judge to sum up the law before the attorneys make their final address to the jury.

Jurors are required to be able both to read and write. We have already described the somewhat tortuous business of jury selection on the *voir dire*. Suffice to say that both the peremptory challenge and the challenge for cause are used extensively by prosecution and defence lawyers in America.

France

Serious offences carrying five or more years of imprisonment are tried by three judges and a jury of nine. In effect there is a more limited use of jury trial in France than in England where only offences carrying more than six months' imprisonment may be tried before a jury.

Jurors must be French citizens aged between 23 and 69. They are drawn from the electoral roll at random. It is a requirement that jurors are able to read and write as in most American States but not in England where illiteracy or innumeracy are not a bar to service.

A defendant has five peremptory challenges and the prosecution, four. As an aid to the use of the challenge, defendants may be provided with the jury panel list before the trial commences. This contrasts with the position in England where the peremptory challenge has recently been abolished and there is talk of proscribing the right of defendants to see a copy of the jury panel list.

Jurors are allowed to ask questions subject to the consent of the senior judge and in general terms there seem to be commendably few rules of evidence. Both judges and jurors retire together to decide the verdict. A guilty verdict must be supported by a majority of at least 8–4. Unusually, judges and jury consider sentence together.

Hong Kong

Throughout the Commonwealth and other British dominions there has been a practice of using smaller juries. Hong Kong has a jury of seven. In the late 1940s diverse countries such as Aden (7) Ceylon (7) the Falklands Islands (7) Jamaica (7) Dominica and Mauritius

(9), and Nyasaland (5) all maintained smaller juries except in capital cases, where generally, but not exclusively, it was twelve (Fiji and Ceylon each had juries of seven).

In Hong Kong the jury system is somewhat unusual; although the common language is Cantonese and only 1% of the population speak English, trials are conducted in English. The effect of this arrangement (which may be necessary) is that jurors are drawn from a narrow section of society: middle-class and educated. Thus the vast majority of defendants are not tried by their peers.

The other odd feature of jury trial in Hong Kong relates to the right to elect trial. Cases may be tried in the District Court before a judge sitting alone and more serious cases are tried in the High Court by a judge and a jury. The great majority of cases may be tried in either court but the choice lies solely with the prosecution.

It is difficult to draw any useful conclusions from comparing these different forms of jury trial. Each system has developed over a period of time in response to many factors which may be peculiar to each country. Most systems have attractive features but it seems unlikely that any aspect of a given system which is more than merely peripheral could find acceptance elsewhere. What then, are the non-jury alternatives?

Laymen sitting with judges

Knittel and Seiler have examined in some detail the workings of the German *Schoeffengericht*.[33] Here two laymen sit with the judge. In more serious trials a judge will sit with two legal observers and two *Schoeffen*. A two-thirds majority is necessary to convict. The *Schoeffen* are intended to be representative of the community, though this is a little optimistic since they are nominated by local worthies for a place on the list of lay judges. They are chosen for particular trials by ballot. Once on the list of *Schoeffen* they tend to sit for about two weeks every year.

Knittel and Seiler question the value of the *Schoeffen's* opinion since they sit with the judge. They argue that although on occasions the laymen may outvote the judge, they lose their candour in his presence.

Professor Cornish has championed the merits of the combined court of judge and jury retiring together, but it seems to us that the presence of a lawyer is inhibiting to the layman. In Russia where two laymen sit with a judge, academics have sought to have the number of laymen increased so they are not overpowered by the presence of the professional judge. In this respect we note the recent observations of one Russian judge who had this to say: 'defendants were invariably convicted at the trial'.[34] It is a scenario that English and American lawyers would find hard to accept.

A similar court structure was proposed fairly recently for England by the Law Society. It was envisaged that a legally qualified chairman sitting with two lay justices might be a suitable tribunal to try a middle range of offences. The right of jury trial was to be preserved. The scheme did not find favour principally because of the cost and the difficulty of finding sufficient numbers of qualified chairmen. It was, however, an idea which appealed to some academics. Professor Glanville Williams, in particular, has recently advocated such a reform in the letters page of *The Times*.[35] If such a concept were introduced it would suffer from the same defects as the *Schoeffen* and their variants. However, it should be added that at the present time appeals from the magistrates are by way of rehearsing before a judge and two magistrates; while this tribunal is generally regarded as only slightly better than a trial before justices, the anecdotal evidence of judges suggests that they find their lay colleagues something of a handful.

Judge alone
It is often said in the legal profession that the ideal tribunal for a lawyer running a solid as opposed to a speculative legal defence is a good stipendiary magistrate – the nearest thing the English criminal justice system has to a judge sitting alone.

In some respects this system has much to recommend it and it is used frequently in America and Canada. It is certainly cheaper than jury trial, and quicker; much of the time now spent in legal argument while the jury sits in its room would be obviated. There is no summing up and counsel's speeches are shorter. If the stipendiary thinks the accused should be acquitted at a fairly early stage he may stop the trial at once. Balanced against this are the arguments that a judge may become case-hardened, biased, or subject to political and peer pressures. Professor Cornish has suggested that it would be undesirable for serious cases to be tried by one person. Certainly in Northern Ireland, where circumstances are admittedly very different, one of the obvious consequences of the suspension of jury trial is the marked fall in acquittal rates.

A bench of three judges

If one is not sufficient then what about three finely trained minds? Would this overcome fears of irrational prejudice and peer pressure? One has in mind Professor Griffith's work, *The Politics of the Judiciary*, which indicates that most judges come from a very narrow social bracket and that their background has a significant influence on their outlook. In these circumstances three judges are little better than one.

In Spain the most serious range of criminal cases are heard by a bench of three judges but as the workload is divided in this country the expense might well be prohibitive. It might be said that expense ought not to be a factor but it cannot be ignored entirely; three judges with pensions, holidays, and sickness benefits all to be paid for would be a considerable burden on the public purse.

Another problem would be recruiting sufficient judges of the necessary calibre. The Beeching Committee commented on the difficulties posed by our system of using part-time judges. Only short cases may be assigned to them for the ten days that they sit. If toward the end of their period a three-day case comes before them it has to be stood over.

Finally, there is the problem of patronage which is a feature of the English judicial system. Full-time appointments are made after consultations with many varying agencies including the presiding judge where the deputy has been sitting. It is difficult enough for the aspiring judge in the present circumstances. Sitting with a senior judge might well inhibit a junior appointee.

Chapter 10

Change or Decay

As this book was finished there were waves of reports relating to juries and their behaviour both in and out of court. Within a matter of months three separate major incidents occurred and they, in turn, were surrounded by a spate of more minor but still troublesome occurrences.

Jury misbehaviour

The first incident was really a by-product of probable police misbehaviour, and indeed served to divert some of the criticism which might otherwise have been levelled more strongly against the prosecution. The police in London had mounted a series of undercover operations to try to infiltrate and smash gangs of football hooligans who were nominally attached to major, mainly first division football clubs, such as West Ham and Chelsea. After one trial had been in progress for some weeks it was announced that the prosecution could not rely on the officers' logbooks kept in the case. The defendants were acquitted on the direction of the judge. So far the case was unremarkable. It then became known that the jury had been out celebrating with the defendants and announced that they had in any event disbelieved the police and found the accused to be jolly good sports. One young member of the jury announced that she was going to date one of the former defendants.[1]

Although there was nothing unlawful in their behaviour, it brought down the wrath of some sections of the press on that particular jury. It was also used as an opportunity to examine what some saw as an example of the general disregard the modern jury has for its role and duties. Fenton Bresler even offered the example of having seen the foreman of a jury wearing tight blue jeans and condemned this as an example of a lack of respect.[2] It appears that comfortable clothing should be eschewed in favour of stiff white collars and a generally respectful lock-pulling attitude to the majesty of the court.

More recently in the autumn of 1989 a trial at the Old Bailey was halted after a juror refused to return to court for the second day of the case. The trial, he said, was 'not his scene'. The entire jury was discharged at a total cost to the taxpayer of £7,200. The juror was fined £100. It was the second case of its kind within a week. Only a few days previously, another juror left the trial on which he was sitting. Boredom was his excuse, for which he was fined £100.

Intimidation

A more disturbing problem was brought into sharp relief in another football hooligan trial, this time in Leeds. It seems that some members of the jury were said to have been intimidated by individuals in the public gallery. The matter was reported to the trial judge who gave, much to the delight of the media, directions to the jurors to pull themselves together and display some resolute character, something described by *The Daily Telegraph* as 'manifestly lacking amongst those chosen to sit in the jury box for this particular trial'. The media devoted little or no attention to the individuals who were said to be responsible for intimidating this particular jury. The trial judge, Jonathan Crabtree, took a no-nonsense view: 'Society's only safeguard is a police force prepared to do its duty and juries having the guts to do what they think is right regardless of the consequences.'[3]

No protection had been offered although it appears that the jury felt it had been the subject of hostile stares from the public gallery throughout the trial. Even if this is so it would not seem to be an instance of professional jury nobbling, rather behaviour that a stern word early in the trial might well have stopped.

Until the English football hooligans departed for the European football championships (thereby providing a diversion) newspapers continued to focus their immediate attention on the jury, its relevance, and its ability to cope in the latter part of the twentieth century. In a third incident jurors in a rape case told the court that there had been an attempt to intimidate them. They were told by Judge

James Rant QC to: 'Do your duty as you have sworn on oath to do. Bring in a true verdict according to the evidence and regardless of the consequences.'[4]

More worrying are the views of Assistant Commissioner John Dellow who has publicly indicated that at least two or three jury nobbling gangs are operating in the London area. This is a view that is shared by other senior police officers, although the scale of the problem is unclear. One senior officer put it in these terms: 'There is a firm in London specialising in jury nobbling and they have got it down to a fine art.'[5]

Apparently a number of jurors have been approached with threats or bribes. In one recent robbery trial at the Old Bailey the jury was discharged after a woman juror reported that she had been offered £5,000 to secure an acquittal. To a great extent elimination of the disease is dependant upon the integrity of individual jurors who speak out when attempts are made to interfere with them or their colleagues. It may be that few have done so and the problem is rife, or if most approaches are reported the instances of jury interference are not that numerous.

It is certainly true that throughout the year there are always, usually in London, one or two juries under police protection. Figures given by the police show that protection costs £68,000 per jury per week. The Metropolitan Police expended 5,500 man days in providing jury protection in the first six months of 1988.[6]

Concrete evidence of jury nobbling is hard to come by, and there have been no successful prosecutions of 'nobblers' in recent years. There is, however, a school of thought amongst the upper echelons of the legal profession which believes the scale of jury nobbling has been greatly exaggerated. It must also be remembered that for every jury to whom an approach is made there are literally thousands which go about their business in a perfectly satisfactory way.

Personation

In 1972 Knittel and Seiler said that 'there are still only a few lawyers in England who venture to suggest the complete abolition of the jury'. What would they have said about the allegations made recently that jurors who did not wish to answer their summonses had been sending, on a fairly wide scale, deputies to sit in their place? It appears that throughout 1987 jurors who were unwilling to honour the summons had been using either friends, relations, or employees to take their place. The evidence of this revival of personation remains anecdotal and relates to south-west London.[7]

A police investigation into this outbreak of personation has failed to identify any individuals involved. There have in fact only been two verified cases in recent years. Significantly, however, the Lord Chancellor's department has taken steps to notify jurors of possible identity checks and of the penalties of personation. Also, in an effort to diminish the motive for personation, the 1973 Practice Direction on random selection has been revoked and reissued with one notable addition that 'jurors may be excused on grounds of personal hardship or conscientious objection to jury service. Each such application should be dealt with sensitively and sympathetically'.[8] This may seem like a common sense measure but it represents a significant shift in the stated policy of the courts.

This issue bears out the view of Professor Cornish that 'the jury system is becoming increasingly controversial'. That much has been proven to be true, particularly since the abolition of the property qualification.

Libel awards

The use of juries in civil trials is rare and beyond the scope of this work. None the less it is difficult to ignore the controversy generated by a spate of libel actions in the last two years. In a series of trials, juries awarded damages against a number of popular daily newspapers. Koo Stark received £300,000, Jeffrey Archer £500,000, and Sonia Suttcliffe £600,000.

Not surprisingly, discontent was expressed most vocally by those newspapers which had unsuccessfully defended libel actions. Setting aside considerations of free speech, a major argument advanced is that some of the libel awards exceed those handed down by judges in the most serious of personal injury cases. On the other hand these juries had some precedent for this level of award; lawyers acting for singer Elton John had only recently persuaded the *Sun* newspaper into agreeing a libel settlement of £1,000,000. There is also a school of thought that the successively higher libel awards represent growing public dissatisfaction with newspapers which choose to gratuitously invade the privacy of individuals for gain. In any event the libel trial which attracted most attention was brought by Sonia Suttcliffe (for-

mer wife of the so-called Yorkshire Ripper) against the satirical magazine *Private Eye*. The award of £600,000 represented a record sum
of damages.* Reporting of the case plumbed new depths as certain
sections of the press took the trial jury to task.

Regrettably it has become commonplace for juries in civil or criminal trials to find themselves the subject of unmeasured criticism. Criticisms of the jury system have tended to be voiced (with certain notable
exceptions) in an increasingly shrill and sometimes uninformed manner. Incidents such as these, though isolated, have focused attention
even more sharply on the jury. Suggestions advocating its total abolition or substantial reform have grown.

Resisting a drift away from jury trial

The last decades, both here and in Northern Ireland, have shown
that once the right of trial by jury is lost, even if it is only intended
to be a temporary measure, it is next to impossible to have it restored.
The advantages to the executive are too many for that to be easily
achieved and the public, presented with a *fait accompli*, effectively
takes no further interest.

We have already noted the practise of prosecutors manipulating
charges to avoid jury trial and the successive measures transferring
cases away from juries to magistrates. The Criminal Justice Act 1988
is yet another measure transferring offences to the magistrates, and
the print on the paper was hardly dry when information was leaked
to *The Times* indicating that: 'senior officers in the Lord Chancellor's
Department are drawing up proposals to be put to ministers, for
restricting the right to trial by jury'.[9]

One other development of note has come about as a result of the
decision in *Stafford* v. *DPP*.[10] In this case it was decided that where
fresh evidence was brought in an appeal against conviction, it was
open to the Court of Appeal to assess this evidence itself rather than
ordering a retrial before a judge and jury. This decision has been
severely criticised by Lords Devlin and Scarman,[11] not least because
issues of fact in criminal trials are the province of juries, not judges.

The decision in the *Stafford* case means that in cases where fresh
evidence comes to light after conviction, defendants are not retried
by a jury but by the Court of Appeal. Effectively what happens is

---

* A settlement of £60,000 was later agreed between the parties.

that the Court weighs the fresh evidence and then considers whether this evidence would have made a difference to the deliberations of the trial jury. Arguably, this extraordinary procedure has contributed to public unease over a number of unsuccessful appeals in recent years. The Court of Appeal has heard fresh evidence in a number of cases, notably the Guildford bombings case, the 'Birmingham Six' and the Carl Bridgewater murder cases. In the Guildford appeal in 1977, the Court of Appeal rejected compelling fresh evidence and upheld the convictions. The appellants remained in custody for a further twelve years before dramatic new evidence made it plain that the Court of Appeal had made a dreadful error.

We believe that the withdrawal of the right of trial by jury (as has been amply demonstrated in the 1930s in Europe) is a symptom of a shift towards dictatorial government. Without the right of trial by jury the rank and file of the population will cease to believe in a system where their cases can be heard only by what they have long thought of as police courts. At such courts it is believed correctly in practice, if wrongly in law, that the burden of proof is on the defendant rather than the State. Without the right to jury trial it will be difficult to maintain the confidence of the public in the legal system.

A drift away from jury trial should be resisted until the necessity for such changes is clearly established. Such a need has not yet been made out. Many of the criticisms levelled at jurors and the jury system have been misinformed, speculative, or worse. Above all, research, comment, and debate on the future of the jury has suffered from a lack of first-hand evidence. If the jury system is not working it is in the public interest that this be made known. If the jury system is capable of improvement it is in the public interest that this be done.

Improving the jury

There are real objections to replacing the jury as we know it; if only because the advantages of the jury system are only really apparent when the alternatives are considered. We now turn to improvements which can and indeed must be made if the jury is to survive the next decade.

Juror protection

The first is a simple, practical point. The jury must be protected from the isolated incidents of intimidation which occur. Court-rooms must be redesigned so that the jury cannot become the focus of abuse or hostility from the public gallery. A repositioning of the jury-box would seem to be the answer. Indeed at some courts where major trials take place (notably the Old Bailey) this has already occurred and the jury-box has been placed under the public gallery. The Lord Chancellor and the Metropolitan Police Commissioner, Sir Peter Imbert, would appear to be taking steps to bring about the general implementation of this simple but necessary step. They have also adopted a number of other reforms including spot checks to identify and eliminate disqualified jurors and personation. It has also been suggested that the Juries Act 1974 Section 5 (which provides for facilities for parties to inspect the panel) should be repealed or amended.

Is there also a case for sequestering a jury from the start? There is little doubt that in the days when the jury was sequestered in capital trials this bred resentment amongst the members. Now that trials have lengthened to the extent that the retirement of the jury can be as long as many of the trials conducted in previous decades, this would seem to be uneconomic and disruptive, certainly in all but the most troublesome cases. In America, except in major cases, the jury is allowed to roam free after retiring to consider its verdict. This also does not seem to be a desirable state of affairs.

Should the jury be sequestered at any time after the commencement of the trial but before it retires to consider its verdict? A case can be made out for the half-way house of contingent sequestration. In simple terms if either party to a trial could prove to the trial judge that there had been an attempt to interfere with the jury he could consider whether to discharge the jury or whether it should be sequestered for the remainder of the trial.

Juror education

One of the complaints voiced by many jurors is that they were not informed of what was going on and what, if any, were their rights. One way of dealing with this would be to ensure that potential jurors watch part or all of a trial before they sit for the first time. This would deal at least with the 'new juror' syndrome. Simply stated this means that jurors on their first trial (for reasons that are easy to understand) are notoriously prone to acquit. It seems inequitable that a defendant's prospects of an acquittal should depend on a fluke allocation of a fresh jury or one wise to its task.

In America in the late 1930s there were schools for jurors. The first was opened in the Post Office Building in Newark, New Jersey. The first class was attended by some 150 men and women; about 2,500 people, mostly women, passed through its portals in the eleven months it remained open. At the very least it would seem to us that a pamphlet should be prepared and sent out with the jury summons to all jurors, explaining just what happens in a trial, and why. The leaflet that currently accompanies the jury summons is both spare and dull.

In America, that legal Garden of Eden, children in sixth grade are taught basic rights and obligations of citizenship. In this country we tend to muddle by. Better education of our children about the responsibility of citizenship (including jury service) might have a beneficial medium and long-term effect.

Juror selection

The aim must be to obtain a panel of thoughtful and unbiased members. Whilst we do not retract our view that vetting is, in almost all cases, an anathema, we believe that without some form of challenge this object is difficult to achieve. The present obsessional belief that random selection is a synonym for lack of bias is impossible to sustain. Only recently one senior judge described our system of selection as 'a lottery within a lottery'. It is foolish to ignore the fact that random selection of jurors may throw up individuals who are constitutionally incapable of carrying out the proper functions of a juror through, for instance, bigotry, illiteracy or ill health.

We advocate therefore, a limited form of *voir dire* to ensure that jurors are at least fluent in English and where necessary, able to read and write. In passing, we would say that there seems to be no reason why illiteracy ought to be a bar where the issues do not require the study of documents. The *voir dire* might also assist in ensuring that jurors are not hopelessly prejudiced for or against the police or some other section of society. We do not think that such a *voir dire* need prove to be particularly time-consuming or expensive. In any event the *voir dire* is infinitely preferable to jury vetting.

Verdict, sentence, and riders

We have already made a case in favour of the abolition of the majority verdict on the ground that it represents a substantial inroad into the burden of proof. It is now clear, however, that the pressing motives behind the introduction of majority verdicts in 1967 had little to do with jury nobbling but rather with issues of cost, efficiency, and a more 'acceptable' conviction rate. That being so it seems unlikely in the present climate that a return to the unanimity rule will find favour in Government circles, especially since there has been no clear-cut fall in public confidence in jury verdicts which can be attributed to majority verdicts.

As to sentence it has long been accepted in this country that this ought not to be the concern of the jury (though we have already said that in Texas, California, and certain European jurisdictions the jury takes an active part in the sentencing process). We do not think this is appropriate in the system as it has evolved in this country, nor would it find acceptance. There was a time, particularly in capital cases, when juries tried to play a role in the sentencing process by urging leniency. More often than not, these were ignored. When they were considered, the trial judge was often invited by the Home Office to give his opinion on the quality and intelligence of the jurors.[12] These days, however, jury riders are all but history.

The abolition of capital punishment has itself obviated the most pressing reason for juries seeking to add riders to verdicts. We have already observed that the power of the coroner's jury to add riders was abolished in 1980. This came about as a result of a series of inquests into deaths during arrest or in police custody. A number of deaths had become a source of public disquiet, notably those of Liddle Towers (1976) and Jimmy Kelly (1979). The culmination of this line of cases was the inquest into the death of Blair Peach in 1980. Blair Peach met his death the previous year at Southall during an anti-National Front demonstration at which there had been violent clashes between demonstrators and members of the Police Special Patrol Group. Scores of demonstrators were beaten and injured. Although the Inquest jury returned a verdict of death by misadventure, it added riders which were severely critical of the police. Within weeks, Parliament abolished the right of Coroner's juries to add such riders.[13] And we note in passing that the following year Parliament enacted Section 8 of the Contempt of Court Act: there is strong argument that the effect of this section outlaws jury riders in any proceedings. It seems that our much-hallowed jury rights are to be admired but no longer used.

There are obvious and good reasons why jurors should be free to add riders if they so wish, particularly where jurors have been considering a case for some days or even weeks and may very well have some useful contribution to make. However, the prospect of reversing the trend we have outlined seems slim.

Repeal of Section 8 of the Contempt of Court Act 1981

We have already discussed in Chapter 9 the circumstances in which Section 8 came into being, thereby effectively closing down any possibility of developing further research into the jury – perhaps by canvassing the views of jurors.

The policy underlying Section 8 has been described as protecting the finality of verdicts. That, of course, is one of the beauties of the jury system: it resolves society's disputes in a single decisive action. There are, however, three arguments in favour of the amendment of repeal of the Section.

Firstly, to establish as a matter of fact how well the jury is functioning. To what extent do juries return verdicts in accordance with the evidence? What can we learn about the decision-making process amongst jurors? Are decisions the product of rational discussion or do two or three control the debate whilst the others acquiesce? To what extent do emotion and prejudice play a part in juror deliberations? Are bargains struck: 'OK, guilty to count one and two but not guilty to count three'?

Secondly, it is necessary to establish whether the Bench and Bar are effectively communicating to juries legal concepts and directions relating to such matters as the burden and standard of proof, corroboration, and the evidence of accomplices. Indeed it is essential to know how juries are applying these concepts and how better to communicate these concepts to the average juror.

Thirdly, if only in view of the Roskill proposals to dispense with juries in cases of complex fraud, it is necessary to obtain firm evidence as to whether juries are able to cope with the evidence in such trials. We note in passing that the evidence on which the Roskill Committee relied in reaching its conclusion that many jurors were 'out of their depth' in fraud trials was based on two pieces of evidence. The first, 'the promptings of common sense', and secondly, evidence given by the applied psychiatry unit at Cambridge (akin to mock jury research). On the face of it the Roskill proposals seem like sound common sense but it is thin evidence on which to abolish a constitutional right.

Every serious researcher into the jury has sought access to the secrets of the jury-room. Kalven and Zeisel managed to make tape-recordings of actual jury deliberations. When this came to light there followed, in their words, 'public censure by the Attorney-General of the United States, a special hearing before the Sub-Committee on Internal Security of the Senate Judiciary Committee, the enactment of statutes in some 30-odd jurisdictions prohibiting jury tapping, and for a brief, painful moment, widespread editorial and news coverage'.[14]

Their desire to get first-hand evidence of the jury was, however, one shared by Professors Cornish, Baldwin and McConville, and McCabe and Purves. Each of these British researchers has had to be content with either testing the verdicts of juries by reference to other participants in the trial process (Baldwin and McConville), by the use of mock and shadow juries (McCabe and Purves), or simply by anecdotal evidence (Cornish). This thoroughly unsatisfactory state of affairs means that effective research into the function of the jury has ground to a halt at a time when it is, perhaps, more desirable than ever. We suggest that, subject to properly safeguarding the anonymity of jurors, defendants, and witnesses, academic researchers could properly be given access to jury deliberations. Taping a jury in session may be an extreme measure inhibiting frank discussion by juries, but canvassing the views of jurors after a verdict has a legitimate and necessary place in research.

Conclusions

As we said at the start of this book, society is undergoing a crisis of confidence in jury trial. In part, this crisis is a product of straightforward and genuine concern as to the efficacy of jury trial in an increasingly complex society. The crisis has been exacerbated by the limited resources which successive administrations have been able or prepared to devote to our system of criminal justice. To a large degree, the crisis has been heightened, even engineered, by many of the detractors of jury trial who have played on the fears and prejudices of the public at every opportunity. To this end allegations of nobbling jurors, packing juries, and the occasional suggestion of impropriety by defence lawyers have been employed. On other occasions the hostility of the opponents of jury trial has been cloaked in apparently altruistic arguments relating to cost, delay and the quality of justice.

Finally, a word about future reforms. In the course of this book we have tentatively suggested for discussion a number of proposals for reform. These proposals have not been made lightly. We have judged each by the criteria that they are necessary or desirable to ensure the continuation of jury trial in a manner that metes out justice between the individual and the State. Yet we would be prepared to be persuaded or to compromise on all but one: that any further reforms of the jury system are preceded by adequate research. Otherwise we are afraid that the jury system will be tinkered with until it becomes unrecognisable. Until there is concrete evidence that the jury system is extensively flawed any such further changes should be put to one side.

Appendix 1:

The Bettaney Letter

Stuart Bell, MP   HMP Brixton
Vice Chairman   1 Jebb Avenue
Labour Home Affairs Committee   London SW2
House of Commons
London, SW1

9 March 1984

Dear Mr Bell,
   Perhaps I may begin by referring you to Mr Tony Dawes' front-page
article in the 'Daily Express' of 17 February, reporting my pre-trial hearing
before the Lord Chief Justice on 16 February?
   In his article Dawes reports your concern over the secrecy surrounding
my forthcoming trial and mentions your intention of writing to the Lord
Chancellor for further details. Since I have little doubt that any such
application will be refused, I am writing to you in order to set out the
decisions taken at the pre-trial hearing:

   (a) The panel of prospective jurors eligible to hear my case is to be
subjected to vetting. This process, with which I am professionally familiar,
involves record checks to establish whether a juror is a member of or
sympathiser with any subversive party or organisation. (In this context the
'subversive' category extends to members of the Labour Party who are
believed to be associated with MT and other 'extremist' elements in the
Party). These checks are supplemented by 'in-depth' discreet enquiries by
the Special Branch amongst a person's colleagues, workmates, neighbours
and friends with the aim of compiling a dossier on the person's political
and social attitudes, his standing in the community and so forth. In this
area, a man or woman's involvement in the Peace Movement or in
'industrial militancy' might be seen in the eyes of the authorities as

sufficient to debar him or her from jury service in my trial. I need hardly elaborate the sort of ideal social/class profile that lies at the heart of these criteria: so stringent a form of passive rejection of 'unsuitable' jurors constitutes in effect selection of the 'right type of person'.

(b) It was decided that certain crucial documentary exhibits will not be produced at the trial, nor be made available to me for the preparation of my defence, despite the fact that much of the crown's case rests on an interpretation of these documents by an expert from the Security Service. Instead, a selection of expurgated exhibits produced by the Director of Public Prosecutions (with assistance from the Legal Adviser of the Security Service) is all that will be exhibited, (and that only in part), to the jury.

(c) Lord Lane rejected an application by my counsel for leave to brief and produce as a witness for the defence a competent expert to comment on, and where necessary to refute, the value judgements of the Security Service expert. He further ruled that, 'in the interests of national security', my counsel's cross-examination of the crown's witness would be curtailed as need be. This means that even in the framework of a totally secret trial there are areas vital to my defence which my counsel will be forbidden to touch upon.

Having witnessed the hearing in its entirety, I am of the opinion that there is no prospect of my receiving anything approaching a fair trial, and I believe this opinion will be shared by many people of all shades of political opinion. I am at present considering whether, as a matter of principle, it is right for me to take any part in what is little more than a travesty of much vaunted British justice.

I believe that the situation which I have outlined above can only add to the genuine concern which you and no doubt other members of the PLP feel about my case. Naturally the decision to hold even the pre-trial hearing behind closed doors was taken with a view to preventing Parliament and the British people from learning of the manner in which my trial is to be conducted. I can assure you that it is not without significance that my trial takes place at a time when many of the hard-won rights of working people in the public service to organise themselves or even to hold opinions contrary to those of the government are under unprecedented and violent attack. GCHQ is only one example. If you so wish, you have my permission to raise this matter in any forum you feel is appropriate, including in the press and broadcasting media. Finally, if you have any questions relating to this matter or to my case in general you are welcome to write to me or visit me at the prison, though visitors must themselves be vetted first!

Yours sincerely,

MICHAEL BETTANEY

Appendix 2:

Attorney-General's Guidelines on Jury Vetting and the exercise of the Stand-by, together with certain recommendations of the Association of Chief Police Officers

The stand-by

1. Although the law has long recognised the right of the Crown to exclude a member of a jury panel from sitting as a juror by the exercise in open court of the right to request a stand-by or, if necessary, by challenge for cause, it has been customary for those instructed to prosecute on behalf of the Crown to assert that right only sparingly and in exceptional circumstances. It is generally accepted that the prosecution should not use its right in order to influence the overall composition of a jury or with a view to tactical advantage.

2. The approach outlined above is founded on the principles that (a) the members of a jury should be selected at random from the panel subject to any rule of law as to right of challenge by the defence, and (b) the Juries Act 1974 together with the Juries (Disqualification) Act 1984 identified those classes of persons who alone are disqualified from or ineligible for service on a jury. No other class of person may be treated as disqualified or ineligible.

3. The enactment by Parliament of s 118 of the Criminal Justice Act 1988 abolishing the right of defendants to remove jurors by means of peremptory challenge makes it appropriate that the Crown should assert its right to stand by only on the basis of clearly defined and restrictive criteria. Derogation from the principle that members of a jury should be selected at random should be permitted only where it is essential.

4. Primary responsibility for ensuring that an individual does not serve on a jury if he is not competent to discharge properly the duties of a juror rests with the appropriate court officer and, ultimately, the trial judge. Current legislation provides, in ss 9 and 10 of the Juries Act 1974, fairly wide discretions to excuse or discharge jurors either at the person's own request, where he offers 'good reason why he should be excused', or where

the judge determines that 'on account of physical disability or insufficient understanding of English there is doubt as to his capacity to act effectively as a juror'.

5. The circumstances in which it would be proper for the Crown to exercise its right to stand by a member of a jury panel are: (a) where a jury check authorised in accordance with the Attorney-General's Guidelines on Jury Checks reveals information justifying exercise of the right to stand by in accordance with para 9 of the guidelines and the Attorney-General personally authorises the exercise of the right to stand by; or (b) where a person is about to be sworn as a juror who is manifestly unsuitable and the defence agree that, accordingly, the exercise by the prosecution of the right to stand by would be appropriate. An example of the sort of *exceptional* circumstances which might justify stand-by is where it becomes apparent that, despite the provisions mentioned in para 4 above, a juror selected for service to try a complex case is in fact illiterate.

Jury vetting
1. The principles which are generally to be observed are (a) that members of a jury should be selected at random from the panel, (b) the Juries Act 1974 together with the Juries (Disqualification) Act 1984 identified those classes of persons who alone are either disqualified from or ineligible for service on a jury; no other class of person may be treated as disqualified or ineligible, and (c) the correct way for the Crown to seek to exclude a member of the panel from sitting as a juror is by the exercise in open court of the right to request a stand-by or, if necessary, to challenge for cause.

2. Parliament has provided safeguards against jurors who may be corrupt or biased. In addition to the provision for majority verdicts, there is the sanction of a criminal offence for a disqualified person to serve on a jury. The omission of a disqualified person from the panel is a matter for court officials but any search of criminal records for the purpose of ascertaining whether or not a jury panel includes any disqualified person is a matter for the police as the only authority able to carry out such a search and as part of their usual function of preventing the commission of offences. The recommendations of the Association of Chief Police Officers rejecting checks on criminal records for disqualified persons are annexed to these guidelines.

3. There are, however, certain exceptional types of case of public importance for which the provisions as to majority verdicts and the disqualification of jurors may not be sufficient to ensure the proper administration of justice. In such cases it is in the interests both of justice and the public that there should be further safeguards against the possibility of bias and in such cases checks which go beyond the investigation of criminal records may be necessary.

4. These classes of case may be defined broadly, as (a) cases in which national security is involved and part of the evidence is likely to be heard in camera, and (b) terrorist cases.

5. The particular aspects of these cases which may make it desirable to seek extra precautions are (a) in security cases a danger that a juror, either voluntarily or under pressure, may make an improper use of evidence which, because of its sensitivity, has been given in camera, (b) in both security and terrorist cases the danger that a juror's political beliefs are so biased as to go beyond normally reflecting the broad spectrum of views and interests in the community to reflect the extreme views of sectarian interests or pressure group to a degree which might interfere with his fair assessment of the facts of the case or lead him to exert improper pressure on his fellow jurors.

6. In order to ascertain whether in exceptional circumstances of the above nature either of these factors might seriously influence a potential juror's impartial performance of his duties or his respecting the secrecy of evidence given in camera, it may be necessary to conduct a limited investigation of the panel. In general, such further investigation beyond one of criminal records made for disqualifications may only be made with the records of police Special Branches. However, in cases falling under para 4(a) above (security cases), the investigation may, additionally, involve the security services. No checks other than on these sources and no general inquiries are to be made save to the limited extent that they may be needed to confirm the identity of a juror about whom the initial check has raised serious doubts.

7. No further investigation, as described in para 6 above, should be made save with the personal authority of the Attorney-General on the application of the Director of Public Prosecutions and such checks are hereafter referred to as 'authorised checks'. When a chief officer of police has reason to believe that it is likely that an authorised check may be desirable and proper in accordance with these guide-lines he should refer the matter to the Director of Public Prosecutions with a view to his having the conduct of the prosecution from an early stage. The Director will make any appropriate application to the Attorney-General.

8. The result of any authorised check will be sent to the Director of Public Prosecutions. The Director will then decide, having regard to the matters set out in para 5 above, what information ought to be brought to the attention of prosecuting counsel.

9. No right of stand-by should be exercised by counsel for the Crown on the basis of information obtained as a result of an authorised check save with the personal authority of the Attorney-General and unless the information is such as, having regard to the facts of the case and the offences charged, to afford strong reason for believing that a particular juror might

be a security risk, be susceptible to improper approaches or be influenced in arriving at a verdict for the reasons given above.

10. Where a potential juror is asked to stand by for the Crown, there is no duty to disclose to the defence the information on which it was founded; but counsel may use his discretion to disclose it if its nature and source permit it.

11. When information revealed in the course of an authorised check is not such as to cause counsel for the Crown to ask for a juror to stand by but does give reason to believe that he may be biased against the accused, the defence should be given, at least, an indication of why that potential juror may be inimical to their interests; but because of its nature and source it may not be possible to give the defence more than a general indication.

12. A record is to be kept by the Director of Public Prosecutions of the use made by counsel of the information passed to him and of the jurors stood by or challenged by the parties to the proceedings. A copy of this record is to be forwarded to the Attorney-General for the sole purpose of enabling him to monitor the operation of these guidelines.

13. No use of the information obtained as a result of an authorised check is to be made except as may be necessary in direct relation to or arising out of the trial for which the check was authorised.

Recommendations of the Association of Chief Police Officers

1. The Association of Chief Police Officers recommends that in the light of observations made in *R v Mason* [1980] 3 All ER 777, [1981] QB 881 the police should undertake a check of the names of potential jurors against records of previous convictions in any case when the Director of Public Prosecutions or a chief constable considers that in all the circumstances it would be in the interests of justice so to do, namely (i) in any case in which there is reason to believe that attempts are being made to circumvent the statutory provisions excluding disqualified persons from service on a jury, including any case when there is reason to believe that a particular juror may be disqualified, (ii) in any case in which it is believed that in a previous related abortive trial an attempt was made to interfere with a juror or jurors, and (iii) in any other case in which in the opinion of the Director of Public Prosecutions or the chief constable it is particularly important to ensure that no disqualified person serves on the jury.

2. The association also recommends that no further checks should be made unless authorised by the Attorney-General under his guidelines and no inquiries carried out save to the limited extent that they may be needed to confirm the identity of a juror about whom the initial check has raised serious doubts.

3. The association further recommends that chief constables should agree to undertake checks of jurors on behalf of the defence only if requested

to do so by the Director of Public Prosecutions acting on behalf of the Attorney General. Accordingly if the police are approached directly with such a request they will refer it to the Director.

4. When, as a result of any checks of criminal records, information is obtained which suggests that, although not disqualified under the terms of the Juries Act 1974, a person may be unsuitable to sit as a member of a particularly jury the police or the Director may pass the relevant information to prosecuting counsel, who will decide what use to make of it.

Notes

Introduction

1. Cornish (1968); Baldwin and McConville (1979); Devlin, Lord (1976) and Green (1985).
2. Most commentators agree on a figure of 97–98 per cent.
3. Devlin (1976), p. 164.
4. Cornish (1968), pp. 141–8; and see Jackson (1972).
5. See, for instance, Justices' Clerks' Society (1982).
6. For a statement of the arguments against jury trial, see Williams (1979).
7. Justices' Clerks' Society, op. cit.
8. Peter Bruinvel M.P., 1 June 1987, *The Daily Telegraph*.
9. Baldwin and McConville (1979), p. 127; although Sealey and Cornish (1973) found that younger jurors were more likely to acquit.
10. Freeman (1981).
11. Williams (1979), p. 271.
12. The Roskill Report, 8.35.
13. Criminal Justice Act 1967, s. 13.
14. Northern Ireland (Emergency Provisions) Act 1973.

Chapter 1: Origins

1. Holdsworth (1922–3), Vol. 1, pp. 312 *et seq.*
2. For an account of early practices see Holdsworth in general and Green (1985).
3. Archer (1956), p. 168.
4. Maitland, Select Pleas of the Crown (SS) 75.
5. Duncomb (1766), p. 79.
6. Devlin (1976), p. 8.
7. This arose out of the trial of the Seven Bishops (1688) who were charged with, and acquitted of, seditious libel.
8. Lewis (1982), p. 26.

9. Juries Act 1870. This brought the law broadly into line with Scotland where jurors were allowed reasonable refreshment. J.R.Lewis records that in 1857 an Inverness jury drank £17 worth of toddy. And at Stirling the overnight bill for one jury came to £70.
10. Ibid., p. 28.
11. Lambert (1935), p. 97.
12. See Holdsworth (1922–3), Vol. 5, pp. 203 *et seq*.
13. Ibid.
14. Ibid.
15. *Bushell's Case* 124 Eng. Rep. 1006.
16. The Trial of John Lilburne, *State Trials*, Vol. 5.
17. Campbell, Lord (1845), Vol. 3. For a fuller account of the case, see Denning (1986), p. 63 *et seq*.
18. Brown (1951), p. 148.
19. Lewis (1982), p. 29.
20. *Law Quarterly Review* vii 17.
21. For a full description of the gradual development of the jury trial in early modern England, see Green (1985), pp. 105 *et seq*.
22. Ibid.
23. Devlin (1976).
24. Pritt (1938) p. 249.
25. The Mersey Committee (1913), para. 236.
26. Juries Act 1825.
27. Cornish (1973).
28. Morris Committee (1965), paras 45–48.
29. Practice Direction (1973) Cr.App.R.

Chapter 2: The State Against the Jury

1. Devlin (1976).
2. Cmnd 2627.
3. Jackson (1972), p. 391.
4. Williams (1979).
5. McEldowney (1977) and (1979)
6. Webb B. and Webb S. (1906), p. 597.
7. Brown, J. (1882).
8. Harman & Griffiths (1979).
9. Thompson (1979).
10. Winslow (1975).
11. Supreme Court Act 1981, s. 76.
12. Thompson (1979), p. 509.
13. TS/11 PRO Ch. Lane (brought to our attention by Campbell & Jeffries, 'Fiddling with Juries', *New Statesman* 1979).
14. Harding, A. (1973).
15. State Trials 1554.
16. State Trials 1664.
17. Thompson (1978).

18. Bentham (1821).
19. McEldowney (1979).
20. McEldowney (1977).
21. Bentham (1821), pp. 210–12.
22. Thompson (1979).
23. Bellamy (1970).
24. Bentham (1821). p. 14.
25. *The Times*: (a) 20 February 1989, *R. v. Berrada* (judge's duty to sum up impartially). (b) 14 June 1989, *R. v. Marr* (defendant's right to fair presentation of case). (c) 23 June 1989, *R. v. Renshaw* (judge's interruptions made trial unfair).
26. Bentham (1821), p. 14.
27. The best account of this period has been written by T.A. Green in *Verdict According to Conscience*.
28. Thompson (1979), p. 150.
29. Malcolmson.

Chapter 3: Vetting

1. *Hansard*, 3 February 1986, Written Answers, cols 55–56.
2. Bresler (1965), p. 114.
3. Rolph (1987).
4. *Hansard*, House of Lords Debates, vol. 358, col. 584 and *Hansard*, Oral Answers, November 1973, col. 26.
5. Cornish (1968) records that, in the summer of 1966, Lord Dilhorne revealed that, when prosecuting a spy trial, he had stood-by a juror whom he knew to have been a communist. Of contemporary commentators only Professor Cornish seems to have worked out the implications.
6. Robertson (1976).
7. *The Times*, 11 October 1978. The Guidelines were subsequently revised on 3 February 1986 and 29 November 1988.
8. For a full account of this case, see Pickles (1987), p. 183.
9. Freeman (1981).
10. Hewart LJ in *R. v. Sussex JJ* (1924) 1 K.B. 259.
11. *Hansard*, House of Lords, Oral Answers, 15 May 1987, cols 415–16. Defence solicitors requested to see the jury panel in only 34 cases in a two-year period between November 1982 and November 1984.
12. *Hansard*, Oral Answers, 15 November 1978, col. 405.
13. Leigh (1979).
14. *Time Out*, 18 January 1980.
15. *The Guardian*, 26 September 1987.
16. Findley & Duff (1988).

Chapter 4: Challenge

1. Radice (1975).
2. For a summary of the relevant authorities, see Archbold, pp. 397–8.

3. Brown, A. (1951), pp. 150–2.
4. For a detailed discussion of the issues, see Dashwood (1972) 'Juries in a Multi-Racial Society' in *Criminal Law Review*.
5. (1970) *Criminal Law Review*, p. 155.
6. (1982) *Criminal Law Review*, p. 522.
7. R. v . *Bansal* (1985) *Criminal Law Review*, p. 151.
8. R. v. *Fraser* (1987) *Criminal Law Review*, p. 418.
9. R. v. *Royston Ford, The Times*, 31 July 1989.
10. Juries Act 1974, s. 5.
11. (1857) 8 E & B 37, p. 81.
12. R. v. *Kray and others* (1969) 53 Cr. App. 412.
13. *New Law Journal*, January 1987.
14. Unpublished address to the National Council of Civil Liberties.
15. Central Criminal Court, 1987.
16. The Attorney-General's Guidelines on jury vetting and the exercise of the stand-by are reproduced in Appendix 2.
17. *New Law Journal*, op.cit.
18. Mark (1979), p. 268.
19. *Hansard*, House of Lords Debates, 21 July 1977, cols 459–462.
20. Baldwin & McConville (1979). Lack of representativeness was a concern also expressed by the Criminal Bar Association paper on jury selection in 1988.
21. Cocks (1986).
22. Vennard & Riley (1988).
23. We have not seen the study but the results are cited by Baldwin & McConville (1979), p. 96.
24. Butler (1985), p. 152–8.
25. Sealey & Cornish (1973), p. 496.
26. For a discussion of jury selection in the Wounded Knee trial, read Christenson (1989). For a discussion on the jury *voire dire* in the Harrisberg trial, see Wrightsman, Kassin & Willis (1987).
27. *The Independent*, 21 April 1989.
28. Hastie, Penrod & Pennington (1983). This contains an even fuller and more entertaining account of the predilictions for types of jurors of American trial lawyers over the last century. It is possible to make a case for or against almost every single ethnic, religious, sex and age group as potential jurors.
29. (1985) 81 Cr. App. R. 217.

Chapter 5: Majority Verdicts

1. Criminal Justice Act 1967, s. 13.
2. Holdsworth (1922–3), Volume I, p. 318.
3. Devlin (1976), p. 56.
4. Stephen (1883), Vol. I, p. 305.
5. Denning (1982), pp. 60–61.
6. *Hansard*, House of Commons Debates, 12 December 1966.

7. For a full description, see Devlin (1976), pp. 50–54.
8. (1952) 36 Cr. App. R. 167.
9. Devlin (1976), p. 56.
10. *Hansard*, House of Commons Debates, 12 December 1966, col. 57.
11. Findley & Duff (1988), p. 213.
12. *Hansard*, House of Lords Debates (Lord Stoneham), 30 July 1968.
13. *R. v. Watson and Others* (1988) 1 All E.R.897.
14. Findley & Duff (1988), p. 192.

Chapter 6: The Rise of the Magistracy

1. *English Justice* (1947) by 'A solicitor'.
2. Quoted by Giles (1963).
3. Webb & Webb (1906), Book 1, p. 558.
4. Babington (1969).
5. Webb & Webb (1906).
6. Geary (1985), pp. 6–24.
7. 10 and 11 c. 82.
8. 11 and 12 Cict. c. 43. Other provisions related to the issue of warrants and summonses as well as costs.
9. Streatfield Report, paras 43, 74, 85 and 112.
10. Cmnd 6323, November 1975.
11. Robert Carr; 6 July 1973. To be fair, the passage continues: 'But we are also conscious of the major issues that would be raised by any proposal to alter the type of case in which there is a right to elect trial'.
12. See, for instance, para. 257.
13. *Hansard*, House of Lords Written Answers, 26 January 1977, col. 601.
14. *Hansard*, House of Lords Written Answers, 13 January 1981, col. 502.
15. Butler (1985), pp. 152–8.
16. *R. v. Harrow JJ, ex p. Osaseri*, 149 J.P.689.
17. *The Times*, 29 July 1988.
18. The Justices' Clerks' Society (1982).
19. Home Office Consultative Document, *The Distribution of Criminal Business* (1986).
20. Particularly Lord Hailsham; see *The Magistrate*, 6 June 1986.
21. Denning (1982).
22. Resolution of the Magistrates' Association; *The Magistrate*, Vol. 37, No. 1, 1986.
23. *The Law Society's Gazette*, 20 May 1986.
24. Justices' Clerks' Society (1982).
25. Harman & Griffiths (1979).
26. *R. v. Davis* (1980) 2 Cr. App. R. (S) 168.
27. *R. v. Turner* (1970) 2 Q.B.321.
28. Baldwin (1985), p. 88.
29. Costs in Criminal Cases Act 1973. See also Levenson (1981).
30. *Hansard*, House of Commons Debates, Vol. 77, 149 2 R. and Vol. 79, 134, 3 R.

31. For a readable personal account of the selection process, see Dadds (1987). For an objective account, see Burney (1979).
32. By the Police and Criminal Evidence Act 1984, s. 76, this procedure now applies to all criminal trials not just those at the Crown Court.
33. *The Law Magazine*, 24 July 1987.
34. Ibid.
35. King & May (1985).
36. Berlins & Dyer (1982), p. 79.
37. King & May (1985), p. 135.
38. Baldwin & McConville (1982), p. 652.
39. *R. v. Bingham JJ ex p. Jowitt, The Times*, 3 July 1974.
40. *The Magistrate*, (1978) Volume 34, p. 28.
41. Burney (1979). Similar problems have been encountered in Scotland; see Bankowski, Hutton & McManus (1987), p. 136.
42. Smith (1983).
43. Hain (1984), p. 129.
44. Lewis (1979).
45. 'Scales of Justice', Yorkshire Television, 4 August 1986.
46. Lewis (1979).
47. Minutes of Evidence to the Royal Commission on the Police (1962), pp. 1300 and 1907.
48. Wolchover, D.
49. The James Committee (1975), para. 24.

Chapter 7: The Roskill Fraud Trials Committee Report

1. Roskill (1986), para. 1.1.
2. Ibid., chapter 1.2 and *Hansard*, House of Commons Debates 1983, Vol. 48.
3. *The Guardian* March 1983.
4. Roskill (1986), Appendix E.
5. Ibid. Chapter 11; Summary of recommendations; Nos. 74–100 inclusive.
6. Ibid., 1.5.
7. Harding (1988), p. 77.
8. Roskill (1986), 8.33 and 8.34.
9. Ibid., 8.35.
10. Ibid., 8.36.
11. Ibid., 9.193.
12. Louis Blom-Cooper Q.C., *The Guardian*, 15 February 1987.
13. See Improving the Presentation of Information to Juries in Fraud Trials.
14. Roskill (1986), 8.15.
15. Ibid., 1.5.
16. Boyle, Hadden & Hillyard (1980).
17. Roskill (1986), 8.65.

Chapter 8: The Suspension of Jury Trial in Northern Ireland

1. The right to vote in local elections was subject to a property qualification. As a result, many individuals usually of the Protestant/loyalist community were entitled to more than one vote. It was no coincidence that a significantly smaller proportion of the Catholic/nationalist population was able to fulfil the qualification. To complete the picture it should be recorded that political control by the loyalist community was maintained, in part, by systematic gerrymandering in both local and national elections. For an excellent analysis of this era, see D. Walsh, *Civil Liberties in Northern Ireland*. See also Cameron (1969) and Scarman (1972).
2. Kelley (1982).
3. The Diplock Commission (1975).
4. Ibid., para. 38.
5. Ibid., para. 35.
6. Hadden & Hillyard (1973), p. 63. This view appeared to be reflected in sentencing in 1973 at least.
7. Diplock (1975), para. 36.
8. Greer and White (1986); letter to *The Independent*, 30 November 1986.
9. Greer and White (1986), p. 78. (Their study is one of the few non-Government studies of the Diplock Court system of any length, and we have drawn on their research for the arguments relating to perverse verdicts and juror intimidation.)
10. This much at least was recognised by Diplock (1975), paras 87–91.
11. Taylor (1980). As Appendix 3, Taylor reproduces a captured IRA document headed 'Staff Report'. Amongst other matter the report deals with educating 'Volunteers' to resist interrogation techniques employed by the security forces.
12. Diplock (1975), para. 17.
13. Boyle, 'Commentaries on the Nothern Ireland (Emergency Provisions) Act 1978', *Current Law Statutes* (1978).
14. *R.* v. *McCormick* (1982) 3 N.I.J.B.
15. Gardiner (1975), para. 26.
16. Baker (1984), paras 104–106.
17. Diplock (1975), para 38.
18. Boyle, op. cit.
19. *The Independent*, 12 August 1987.
20. Bennett (1979), Cmnd 7497.
21. See (a) *Eire* v. *United Kingdom*, E.C.H.R. (1978); (b) conclusions of the Amnesty International Mission to Northern Ireland (1978): 'Amnesty International believes that maltreatment of suspected terrorists by the RUC has taken place with sufficient frequency to warrant the establishment of a public enquiry; (c) Bennett (1979).
22. Greer (1980).
23. Walsh (1984), p. 338.
24. Jennings & Wolchover (1984).

Chapter 9: Jury Trial: Arguments for and against, and the Alternatives

1. Devlin (1976), p. 194.
2. Knittel & Seiler (1972).
3. Blackstone (1979), Vol. IV, p. 343.
4. Cole & Postgate (1966), p. 155.
5. Gifford (1986).
6. Pritt (1938).
7. Evans (1983), pp. 85–94.
8. Jackson (1972), pp. 389–91, and Cornish (1968), p. 138.
9. For a full account, see Denning (1984), pp. 103–18.
10. Criminal Justice Act 1988.
11. Cornish (1968), p. 128.
12. Roskill (1986), 8.28.
13. James Committee (1975), para. 43.
14. The Home Office Consultative Document on the Distribution of Criminal Business, 1986.
15. Justices' Clerks' Society (1982), para 59–66.
16. *New Law Journal*, 9 June 1966.
17. Mark (1979), p. 285.
18. Vennard (1985), p. 142.
19. McCabe & Purves (1972).
20. Zander (1974).
21. Butler (1985).
22. Baldwin & McConville (1979), p. 132.
23. Bystander (1973).
24. Butler (1985).
25. Williams (1979), p. 272.
26. *R.* v. *Chapman and Landay* (1976) 63 Cr. App. R. 750.
27. Deavons (1965), p. 195.
28. *R.* v. *Armstrong* (1921) Cr. App. R.
29. *Ellis* v. *Deheer* [1922] 2 K.B. 113.
30. *Attorney-General* v. *New Statesman and Nation Publishing Co. Ltd* [1980] 2 W.L.R. 246.
31. *The Times* 28 July 1988.
32. Blumberg, p. 55.
33. Knittel and Seiler (1972).
34. 'Haldane Heads East', *Socialist Lawyer* (1989), Spring edition.
35. Correspondence in *The Times*, 5 November 1988.

Chapter 10: Change or Decay

1. *Daily Mirror*, 20 May 1988.
2. *Evening Standard*, June 1988.
3. *The Times*, 2 June 1988.
4. *Daily Mail*, 10 June 1988.

5. *Daily Telegraph*, 30 September 1988.
6. *The Times*, 25 July 1988.
7. Juror personation has an old if not venerable history. There has been a trickle of cases over the last two hundred years involving personation. In *Tremearne* (1826) B & C 254, a juror, Williams, sent his son to serve in his place. In *R* v. *Levy* (1916) Times Law Reports 235, a jury summons for one Frank Levy arrived whilst he was away supervising the family business. His summons was answered by his brother, Bob. In *R.* v. *Wakefield* (1918) 1 K.B. 216, the defendant was convicted on a charge of rape. After the trial it became apparent that one of the jurors was an imposter. The personator, Clark, had gone to court to secure his employer's excusal from jury service on the grounds of age. Somehow, when his master's name was called, Clark answered and took his place in the jury box. The conviction was set aside and a retrial was ordered when Wakefield was acquitted. Clark was less fortunate. He was successfully prosecuted for impersonating a juror, fined a nominal sum and ordered to pay the costs of the prosecution. For a full account, see Enright (1988).
8. *New Law Journal*, 23 September 1988.
9. *The Times*, 25 July 1988.
10. (1973) 3 W.L.R. 719.
11. 'Justice and the Guildford Four', *The Times*, 30 November 1988.
12. Bresler (1965), p. 114.
13. Coroners Amendment Rules 1980.
14. Kalven & Zeisel (1965), p. vii.

Bibliography

Ali, T. (1979) 'The Curtain Falls But the Show Goes On'. *The Guardian*, September 24.

Archbold, *Criminal Pleadings and Practice* (43rd edition, London, Sweet & Maxwell).

Archer, P. (1956) *The Queen's Courts* (Harmondsworth, Penguin).

A Solicitor (1947) *English Justice* (London, Pelican).

Association of Chief Police Officers (1966) 'Analysis of Persons Committed to Assize, Crown Courts and Quarter Sessions During 1965', *New Law Journal*, June 9.

Babington, A. (1969) *A House in Bow Street* (London, Macdonald).

Bailey, S.H., Harris, D.J., and Jones, B.L., (1985) *Civil Liberties* (London, Butterworths).

Baker, G. (1984) *Review of the Operation of the Northern Ireland (Emergency Provisions) Act 1978* (London, HMSO, Cmnd 9222).

Baldwin, J. (1985) *Pre-Trial Justice* (Oxford, Basil Blackwell).

Baldwin, J. and McConville, M. (1978) 'The New Home Office Figures on Pleas and Acquittals – What Sense Do They Make?' *Criminal Law Review*.

Baldwin, J. and McConville, M. (1979a) *Jury Trials* (Oxford University Press).

Baldwin, J. and McConville, M. (1979b) 'The Representativeness of Juries', *New Law Journal*, 23 March, 1979.

Baldwin, J. and McConville, M. (1982) 'The Influence of Race on Sentencing', *Criminal Law Review*,

Bankowski, Z., Hutton, N. and McManus, J. (1987) *Lay Justice* (Edinburgh, Clark).

Barber, D. and Gordon, G. (eds) (1976) *Members of the Jury* (London, Wildwood House).

Beckman, M. and Taylor, C. (1987) 'Judicial Tinkering: Enough is Enough', *The Lawyer*, December 17.

Bellamy, J. G. (1970) The Law of Treason in England in the Later Middle Ages (London, Cambridge University Press).

Bennett, (1979) *Report of the Committee of Enquiry into Police Interrogation Procedures in Northern Ireland* (London, HMSO, Cmnd 7497).

Bentham, J. (1821) *The Elements of the Art of Packing as Applied in Special Juries in Cases of Libel Law* (London, Wilson).

Berlins, M. and Dyer, C. (1982) *The Law Machine* (Harmondsworth, Penguin).

Blackstone (1979) *Commentaries of the Laws of England* (London, University of Chicago Press).

Blom-Cooper, L. (1986) 'Crimes Beyond the Ken of Ordinary Folk', *The Guardian*, February 15.

Boyd, A. (1984) *The Informers* (Dublin & Cork, Mercier Press).

Boyle, K., Hadden, T. and Hillyard, P. (1980) *Ten Years On In Northern Ireland* (London, Cobden Trust).

Bresler, F. (1965) *Reprieve* (London, Harrap).

Brown, Alec (1951) *The Juryman's Handbook* (London, The Harvill Press).

Brown, J. (1882) *Abolition of Trial by Jury*, Bow Legal Pamphlets, Vol. 17 (London, The Bow Group).

Burney, E. (1979) *Magistrates' Courts and Community* (London, Hutchinson).

Butler, S. (1985) *Managing Criminal Justice* (London, HMSO).

Bystander (1973) 'The Guilty are Convicted', *The Law Society's Guardian Gazette*, September/October.

Cameron (1969) *Report of the Commission appointed by the Governor of Northern Ireland* (Belfast, HMSO, Cmnd 532).

Campbell, Lord (1845) *The Lives of the Lord Chancellors*, Vol. 3 (London, John Murray).

Cockerell, M. (1987) 'Punishment in the People's Court', *The Law Magazine*, July 24.

Carlen, P. (1976) *Magistrates' Justice* (London, Martin Robertson).

Christenson, R. (1989) *Political Trials – Gordian Knots in the Law* (Oxford, Transaction Publishers).

Cocks, D. (1986) 'The Sound of Tinkering', *Counsel*, Easter.

Cole, G. and Postgate, R. (1966) *The Common People* (London, Methuen).

Compton, (1971) *Report of the Enquiry into Allegations Against the Security Forces of Physical Brutality in Northern Ireland Arising out of Events on 9 August 1971* (London, HMSO).

Coote, A. (1978) 'The 'Loyal' Jury and the Foreman with Firm Opinions', *New Statesman*, September 2.

Cornish, W.R. (1968) *The Jury* (Harmondsworth, Penguin).

Cornish, W.R. (1973) 'Qualifications for Jury Service', *Criminal Law Review*.

Corporation of London Especial Committee Respecting Juries (1818) Corporation of London Records Office Miscellaneous Manuscripts, 174.3.

Criminal Bar Association (1988) *Jury Selection*.

Criminal Law Revision Committee (11th Report) (London, HMSO, Cmnd 4991).

Dadds, K. (1987) 'Bench Marks Test', *The Guardian*, March 20.
Daily Telegraph, The (1987) 'Trial Halted After £5000 Bribe Bid to Woman Juror', September 30.
Dashwood, A. (1974) 'The Jury and the Angry Brigade', *Western Australian Review*.
Deavons, E. (1965) 'Serving as a Juryman in Britain', 25 *Modern Law Review*.
Denning, Lord (1982) *What's Next in the Law*? (London, Butterworths).
Denning, Lord (1984) *Landmarks in the Law* (London, Butterworths).
Denning, Lord (1986) *Leaves from my Library* (London, Butterworths).
Devlin, Lord (1976) *Trial by Jury* (London, Stevens & Sons).
Devlin, Lord (1988) 'Justice and the Guildford Four', *The Times*, November 30.
Diplock, Lord (1972) *Report of the Commission to Consider Legal Procedures to Deal with Terrorist Activities in Northern Ireland* (London, HMSO, Cmnd 5185).
Dromey, J. and Taylor, G. (1979) *Grunwick: The Workers' Story* (London, Lawrence & Wishart).
East, R. (1985) 'Jury Packing: A Thing of the Past?, 48, *Modern Law Review*.
Enright, S. (1988) 'Britain's Reluctant Jurors', *New Law Journal*, July 29.
Evans, K. (1983) *Advocacy at the Bar* (London, Financial Training).
Fine, B. and Miller, R. (1985) *Policing the Miners' Strike* (London, Lawrence & Wishart).
Findley, M. and Duff, P. (eds) (1988) *The Jury Under Attack* (London, Butterworths).
Fitzgerald, M. and Muncie, J. (1983) *System of Justice* (Oxford, Basil Blackwell).
Frank, J. and Frank, B. (1957) *Not Guilty – 36 Comparatively Recent Cases in Which the Wrong Man was Convicted* (London, Gollancz).
Freeman, M. (1981) 'The Jury on Trial', *Current Legal Problems*.
Gardiner, Lord (1975) *Report of a Committee to Consider in the Context of Civil Liberties and Human Rights, Measures to Deal with Terrorism in Northern Ireland* (London, HMSO, Cmnd 5847).
Geary, R. (1985) *Policing Industrial Disputes* (Cambridge, Cambridge University Press).
Gifford, T. (1986) *Where's the Justice*? (London, Penguin).
Giles, F.T. (1963) *The Magistrates' Courts* (London, Stevens).
Green, T. (1985) *Verdict According to Conscience* (Chicago, Chicago University Press).
Greer, D. (1980) 'The Admissibility of Confessions under the Northern Ireland Emergency Provisions', *Northern Ireland Law Quarterly* Vol. 31.
Greer, S. and White, A. (1986) *Abolishing the Diplock Courts* (London, Cobden Trust).
Griew, E. (1967) 'The Behaviour of the Jury: a Review of American Evidence', *Criminal Law Review*.

Guardian, The (1979) 'What the Police Computer Said About 19 Jurors', September 20.

Hadden, T. and Hillyard, P. (1973) *Justice in Northern Ireland* (London, Cobden Trust).

Hain, P. (1984) *Political Trials in Britain* (Harmondsworth, Penguin).

Harding, A. (1973) *The Law Courts of Mediaeval England* (London, George Allen & Unwin).

Harding, R. (1988) 'Jury Performance in Complex Cases', in *The Jury under Attack* (London, Butterworths).

Harman, H. and Griffiths, J. (1979) *Justice Deserted* (London National Council for Civil Liberties).

Hastie, R., Penrod, S.D. and Pennington, N. (1983) *Inside the Jury* (Cambridge, Mass., Harvard University Press).

Hay, D. (1975) 'Property, Authority and the Criminal Law', in *Albion's Fatal Tree* (London, Peregrine).

Helm, S. (1988) 'Passing Judgment on the Jury', *The Independent*, July 3.

Holdsworth, (1922–3) *A History of English Law* (London, Methuen).

Home Office (1986) *White Paper on Criminal Justice* (London, HMSO).

Hone, W. (1823) *The Three Trials of William Hone* (London).

Jackson, R.M. (1972) *The Machinery of Justice in England* (6th edn, London).

James Committee (1975) *The Distribution of Business between the Crown Court and Magistrates Courts* (London, HMSO).

Jennings, A. and Wolchover, D. (1984) 'The Star Chamber versus the Gang of Twelve', *New Law Journal,*

Jennings, A. (ed.) (1988) *Justice Under Fire* (London, Pluto Press).

Jones, A. (1983) *Jury Service* (London, Robert Hale).

Jones, L. (1984) 'Shut Up and Listen', *The New Statesman*, March 2.

Justices' Clerks' Society (1982) *A Case for Summary Trial* (London).

Kalven, H. and Zeisel, H. (1965) *The American Jury* (Boston, Little Brown).

Kelley, K. (1982) *The Longest War* (Ireland, Brownlow Publishers Ltd).

King, M. and May, C. (1985) *Black Magistrates* (London, Cobden Trust).

Knittel, E. and Seiler, D. (1972) 'The Merits of Trial by Jury', *Cambridge Law Journal.*

Lambert, R.S. (1935) *When Justice Faltered* (London, Methuen).

Leigh, D. (1979) 'What the Police Computer Said About 19 Jurors', *The Guardian*, September 20.

Leigh, D. (1980) *The Frontiers of Secrecy* (London, Junction Books).

Levenson, H. (1981) *The Price of Justice* (London, Cobden Trust).

Lewis, J. R. (1982) *The Victorian Bar* (London, Robert Hale).

Lewis, R. (1979) *Real Trouble – A Study of Aspects of the Southall Trials* (London, The Runnymede Trust).

London Chamber of Commerce (1930) *The Curse of Trial by Jury* (Legal Pamphlets).

Malcolmson, 'Infanticide in Eighteenth-Century England', in *Crime in England*, ed. Cockburn.

Mark, R. (1979) *In the Office of Constable* (Glasgow, Collins).

McCabe, S. and Purves, R. (1972) *The Jury at Work* (Oxford, Basil Blackwell).

McCabe, S. and Purves, R. (1974) *The Shadow Jury at Work* (Oxford, Basil Blackwell).

McEldowney, J. (1977) '*The Queen* v. *McKenna* (1869) and Jury Packing in Ireland', *Irish Jurist*, Vol. 12.

McEldowney, J. (1979) 'Stand-by for the Crown', *Criminal Law Review*.

McFarlane, G. (1989) 'Musings on the Jury System', *Solicitors Journal*, March 17.

Medical Research Council (1986) 'Improving the presentation of information to juries in fraud cases' (London, HMSO).

Mersey Committee (1913) (London, HMSO, Cmnd 6817).

Milton, F. (1959) *In Some Authority*, (London, Pall Mall Press).

Moir, E. (1969) *The Justice of the Peace* (Harmondsworth, Penguin).

Monckton, C. (1988) 'Has the Jury Sentenced Itself to Death', *The Standard*, June 3.

Morris Committee (1965) *Report of the Departmental Committee on Jury Service* (London, HMSO, Cmnd 2627).

Moxon, D. (ed.) (1985) *Managing Criminal Justice – A Collection of Papers* (London, HMSO).

NACRO (1987) *Black People and the Criminal Justice System* (London, NACRO).

Pickles, J. (1987) *Straight from the Bench* (London, J.M. Dent & Sons).

Ponting, C. (1985) *The Right to Know* (London, Sphere Books).

Pritt, D.N. (1971) *The Apparatus of the Law* (London, Lawrence & Wishart).

Pritt, D.N. (1938) *A Barrister* (London, Gollancz).

Radevsky, A. (1976) 'Pacifism and the Incitement to Disaffection Act', (unpublished dissertation, University of Southampton).

Radice, B. (ed.) (1975) *Cicero Murder Trials* (Harmondsworth, Penguin).

Radzinowicz, L. (1968) *History of the English Criminal Law*, Vol. IV (London, Stevens & Sons).

Reform of Section 2 Official Secrets Act 1911, (1988) (London, HMSO, Cmnd 408).

Robertson, G. (1976) *Reluctant Judas* (London, Temple Smith).

Robertson, G. (1979) *Obscenity* (London, Weidenfeld & Nicolson).

Rogally, J. (1977) *Grunwick* (Harmondsworth, Penguin).

Rolph, C.H. (1961) *The Trial of Lady Chatterly* (London, Penguin).

Rolph, C.H. (1987) *Further Particulars* (Oxford University Press).

Roskill, Lord (1986) Fraud Trials Committee Report (London, HMSO)

Royal Commission on Justices of the Peace (1910) (London, HMSO)

Scarman, Lord (1972) *Violence and Civil Disturbance in Northern Ireland* (Belfast, HMSO, Cmnd 566).

Scorer, C. (1976) *The Prevention of Terrorism Acts 1974 and 1976* (London, NCCL).

Sealey, A. and Cornish, W.R. (1973) 'Juries and the Rules of Evidence', *Criminal Law Review*.

Sealey, A. and Cornish, W.R. (1973) 'Jurors and their Verdicts', *Modern Law Review*, 36.

Skyrme, T. (1985) *The Changing Image of the Magistracy* (London, Macmillan).

Smith, R. (1983) *The Oxfraud Incident*, Legal Action Group, February.

'Solicitor' (1932) English Justice. (London, Penguin).

Southall, 23 April 1979. *Report of the Unofficial Committee of Enquiry* (London, NCCL).

Stalmaster, I. (1931) *What Price Jury Trials?* (Boston, Stratford).

Stephen, J. (1883) *History of the Criminal Law* (London, Macmillan).

Stevas, N. St John (1956) *Obscenity and the Law* (London, Secker & Warburg).

Streatfield Report (1961) (London, HMSO, Cmnd 1289).

Sunday Times (1973) 'Mysteries of the Jury Room', October 7.

Sunday Times (1973) 'Juries: Trial by Error?', October 28.

Sunday Times (1978) 'Sam Silkin's Whitehall Farce', November 19.

Taylor, P. (1980) *Beating the Terrorists?* (Harmondsworth, Penguin).

Thayer, J.B. (1892) *A Preliminary Treatise on Evidence*

Thompson, E.P. (1977) *Whigs and Hunters* (Harmondsworth, Peregrine).

Thompson, E.P. (1978) 'The State Versus its Enemies', *New Society*, October 19.

Thompson, E.P. (1979) *The Making of the English Working Class* (Harmondsworth, Penguin).

Time Out (1980) 'It Shouldn't Happen to a Jury', January 18.

Times, The (1978) 'Attorney-General's Guideline on Jurors', October 11.

Times, The (1988) 'Law Officers Want to Limit the Right', July 23.

Train, A. (1924) *Courts and Criminals* (New York, Scribners).

Vennard, J. (1985) 'The Outcome of Contested Trials', in *Managing Criminal Justice* (London, HMSO).

Vennard, J. and Riley, D. (1988) 'The Use of Peremptory Challenge and Standby of Jurors and their Relationship to Trial Outcome', *Criminal Law Review*, November.

Wallington, P. (ed.) (1984) *Civil Liberties* (London, Cobden Trust).

Walsh, D. (1984) 'Civil Liberties in Northern Ireland', in *Civil Liberties 1984*, ed. Wallington.

Webb, S. and Webb, B. (1906) *English Local Government* (London, Longmans).

White, R.C.A. (1985) *The Administration of Justice* (Oxford, Basil Blackwell).

Whittington-Egan, R. (1989) *The Riddle of Birdhurst Rise* (London, Penguin).

Whittington-Egan, R. (1989) *The Ordeal of Philip Yale Drew* (London, Penguin).

Williams, G. (1979) *The Proof of Guilt* (3rd edn, London, Stevens).

Winslow, C. (1977) 'Sussex Smugglers', in *Albion's Fatal Tree* (London, Peregrine).

Woffinden, B. (1989) *Miscarriages of Justice* (London, Coronet).

Wolchover, D. (1985) 'The Scandalous Denial of Jury Trial in Assault on Police Cases', *Law Society's Guardian Gazette*, October 24.

Wolchover, D. (1986) 'Police Perjury', *New Law Journal*, February.

Wolchover, D. (1986) 'The Right to Trial', *New Law Journal*, June 3.

Wrightsman, L.S., Kassin, S.M. and Willis, C.E. (1987) *In the Jury Box* (Newbury Park, Calif., Sage Publications Inc.).

Zander, M. (1974) 'Acquittal Rates and Not-Guilty Pleas', *Criminal Law Review* p. 381.

Zander, M. (1974) 'Are Too Many Criminals Avoiding Conviction?' *Modern Law Review* p. 28.

Zander, M. (1988) *Justice in Ferment* (London, I.B. Taurus).

Index